Margaret von Ziegésar / Detlef von Ziegésar

TRAINING

Englische Grammatik

Sekundarstufe II

Beilage: Lösungsheft

Ernst Klett Verlag
Stuttgart Düsseldorf Leipzig

Bildquellen

Cartoons auf den Seiten 18, 19, 27, 45, 57, 67, 77, 78, 81, 105, 115 und 135
aus: D. and R. Manley: The Piccolo Book of Cartoons, Pan 1977
Cartoon auf Seite 35: Express Newspapers 1983
Cartoon auf Seite 69: The Mirror, 21. 9. 1985
Cartoon auf Seite 86: The Mirror, 15. 6. 1985

Gedruckt auf Papier, das aus chlorfrei gebleichtem Zellstoff hergestellt wurde.

Die Deutsche Bibliothek – CIP-Einheitsaufnahme

Ziegésar, Margaret von:
Training englische Grammatik :
Sekundarstufe II / Margaret von Ziegésar ; Detlef von Ziegésar. –
9. Aufl. – Stuttgart ; Düsseldorf ; Leipzig : Klett, 1999
ISBN 3-12-922108-5

9. Auflage 1999

Internetadresse: http://www.klett-verlag.de/klett-lerntraining
Gesamtherstellung: Wilhelm Röck, Weinsberg
Illustrationen: Hitz und Mahn, Stuttgart
Zeichnungen auf den Seiten 10, 49, 57 und 80: Ingo Schimazek, Rheinstetten
Einbandgestaltung: Bayerl & Ost, Frankfurt/M.
ISBN 3-12-922108-5

Inhalt

Einleitung

„Training Englische Grammatik" hilft allen, die die englische Grammatik wiederholen und üben möchten. Das Buch kann man entweder mit einer Lehrkraft oder alleine zu Hause benutzen.
Der Schwerpunkt liegt auf den grammatischen Strukturen, die häufig Schwierigkeiten machen. Wenn Sie glauben, eine grammatische Struktur nicht sicher zu beherrschen, können Sie hier nachschlagen, wiederholen und üben. Das Buch kann natürlich auch als reines Nachschlagewerk benutzt werden.

So arbeiten Sie mit diesem Buch

Sie sollten nicht versuchen, das ganze Buch von vorne bis hinten durchzuarbeiten – schon gar nicht an einem Stück! Statt dessen gehen Sie folgendermaßen vor:

Suchen Sie mit Hilfe des Inhaltsverzeichnisses die grammatischen Gebiete heraus, die Ihnen Schwierigkeiten bereiten.

Arbeiten Sie zuerst den Abschnitt „Überprüfen Sie Ihr Wissen" durch, der immer die einzelnen Grammatikkapitel einleitet. Sie verschaffen sich damit mehr Klarheit darüber, wo Ihre Probleme liegen. Bearbeiten Sie erst alle Aufgaben dieses Abschnittes, bevor Sie Ihre Antworten mit denen im Lösungsheft vergleichen. Dort stehen dann nach allen Antworten Hinweise auf die Kapitelabschnitte, die Ihnen helfen, Ihre Schwierigkeiten zu erkennen und gezielt zu beheben.

Im nächsten Schritt beschäftigen Sie sich mit den von Ihnen ausgewählten Kapitelabschnitten, oder Sie arbeiten das ganze Kapitel vom Anfang bis zum Ende durch – aber bitte nicht an einem Stück! Man lernt viel besser, wenn man immer wieder kleinere Abschnitte bearbeitet und wiederholt, mit vielen Pausen dazwischen.

Lesen Sie die auf den Abschnitt „Überprüfen Sie Ihr Wissen" folgenden Regeln und Beispielsätze aufmerksam durch. Die wichtigsten Merkmale der Regeln sind unterstrichen, damit Sie sich schnell einen Überblick verschaffen können.

Bearbeiten Sie dann die nachfolgenden Übungen. Schließen Sie immer eine Übung ab, bevor Sie Ihre Antworten mit denen im Lösungsheft vergleichen. Wenn Sie glauben, die Regeln immer noch nicht ganz verstanden zu haben, schauen Sie sich die Regeln, Beispielsätze und Übungen noch einmal an. Wenn es aber doch ganz gut geklappt hat, können Sie im Kapitel fortfahren.

Wenn Sie ein Kapitel ganz durchgearbeitet haben, versuchen Sie den Abschnitt „Überprüfen Sie Ihr Wissen" noch einmal. Diesmal dürften eigentlich keine Schwierigkeiten mehr bestehen. Wenn einiges aber immer noch nicht ganz klar ist, machen Sie zunächst eine Pause und schauen sich dann das Kapitel noch einmal an.

Und nun wünschen wir Ihnen viel Erfolg!

1. Simple present – present continuous

In diesem Kapitel wiederholen wir alles, was Sie wissen müssen, um die ***simple present*** und ***present continuous***-Formen richtig anwenden zu können.

Zuerst einige Beispiele für diese zwei Formen:

simple present	present continuous
Ken **works** in a supermarket.	Ken **is working** in York at the moment.
Ann **watches** TV every night.	Ann **is watching** TV.
I **speak** French.	Tony **is learning** Spanish.
Wolfgang **comes** from Germany.	Jill **is staying** with me this week.
The earth **goes** round the sun.	It**'s getting** warmer.
What **happens** in the film?	What**'s happening** outside?
What **do** I **do** next?	You**'re** always **listening** to music.
It **depends** on the weather.	It**'s raining**.
That record **belongs** to me.	Sally **is being** silly today.
How much **do** you **weigh**?	I**'m trying** to eat less.
I **think** you're right.	My brother **is thinking** of going to England.

Prüfen Sie jetzt bitte nach, ob Sie die beiden Zeitformen richtig benutzen können.

Überprüfen Sie Ihr Wissen

Test 1

Es ist sehr wichtig, daß Sie die zwei Formen richtig anwenden können, denn sie verändern die Bedeutung einer Äußerung. Bemerken Sie z. B., welche unterschiedlichen Bedeutungen diese zwei Sätze haben?

a) Margaret **lives** in Sheffield.
b) Margaret **is living** in Sheffield.

Test 2

Choose the simple present or present continuous forms of the verbs in brackets.

1. Would you like some beer? – No, thanks. I ..... alcohol. (not drink)
2. Why ..... you ..... French? (learn) – Because I ..... to go to France next summer. (want)
3. Where ..... you ..... from? (come)
4. What ..... your father ..... for a living? (do)
5. My sister ..... to be a nurse. (train)
6. That's an interesting article. It ..... you all about British teenagers. (tell)
7. What ..... you .....? (read) – A thriller. It's very good.
8. Where ..... I ... a ticket, please? (get)
9. I don't like Mr. Smith. He ..... too much. (talk)
10. Carol, hurry up! What ...... you ..... in the bathroom all this time? (do)
11. How ..... you ..... these days? (get on)
12. What language ..... they ..... in Peru? (speak)
13. I think it ..... colder. We'd better take coats. (get)
14. My uncle ..... always ..... me about girlfriends. (ask)

Im folgenden wiederholen wir alle Regeln, die Sie brauchen, um die zwei Formen richtig anwenden zu können. In den sich anschließenden Übungen können Sie überprüfen, ob Sie die Regeln verstanden haben.

Grammatikregeln und Übungen

§ 1 Gebrauch des simple present

Man verwendet das ***simple present*** für:

Ken **works** in a supermarket. Paul **watches** TV every night. Tony **plays** the guitar in a band. past – now – future	1. Berufsmäßige und sonstige gewohnheitsmäßige Tätigkeiten. Typische Zeitbestimmungen: *every (day), normally, usually, always, never*
My brother only **drinks** milk. I **speak** French and German. My mother **enjoys** thrillers.	2. Typische Eigenschaften, Fähigkeiten und Einstellungen. Typische Verben: *to love, to enjoy, to hate, to like, to allow, to say*
Where **do** you **come** from? I **come** from Germany. The earth **goes** round the sun.	3. Tatsachen und Dauerzustände, die als zeitlos gültig angesehen werden
What **happens** in the film? What **does** Tony **say** in his letter? He **explains** why he can't come to the wedding. The article **deals** with the problems of pollution.	4. Inhaltsangaben (Buch, Film, Brief, Telefongespräch, Zeitungsartikel); Inhalte erfragen; Schlagzeilen
... Jones **passes** the ball to Williams. Williams **runs** towards the goal ... Now watch: First I **pour** the water into the glass. Then I **add** ...	5. Begleitkommentar zu einer Aufeinanderfolge von Handlungen, z. B. Sportreportagen, Experimente, Kochrezepte usw.
What **do** I **do** next? How **do** we **get** to the station? Let me help you to fill in the form: first you **write** your name at the top.	6. Anweisungen und Auskünfte
I was waiting for the bus this morning. Then a man **comes** up to me and **says**...	7. Die lebendigere oder dramatischere Darstellung vergangener Ereignisse

§2 Gebrauch des present continuous

Man verwendet das ***present continuous*** für:

I'm just **doing** my homework.

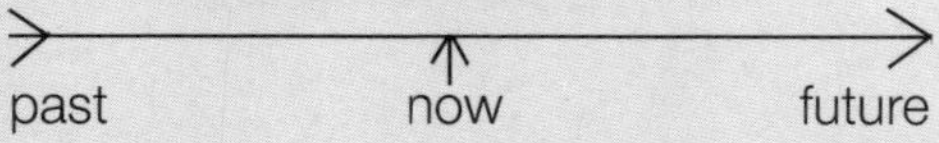

1. Vorgänge, die im Moment des Sprechens ablaufen.
   Typische Zeitbestimmungen:
   just, (just) now, at the moment

Sue **is learning** French.
I'm trying to stop smoking.

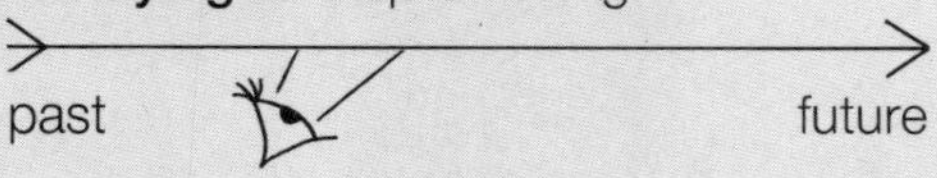

2. Vorgänge, die begonnen haben und noch nicht zu Ende sind, die aber auch gerade unterbrochen sein können. Unser Augenmerk ist auf eine bestimmte Zeitspanne gerichtet.

Jill **is staying** with me at the moment.

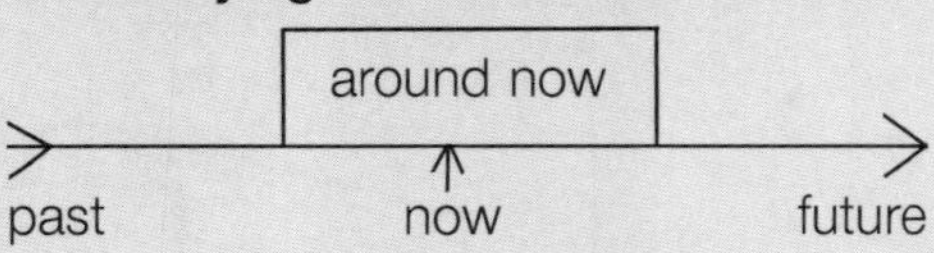

3. Vorgänge, die vorübergehender Natur sind.
   Typische adverbiale Bestimmungen:
   at the moment, these days, this week

The weather **is getting** warmer.

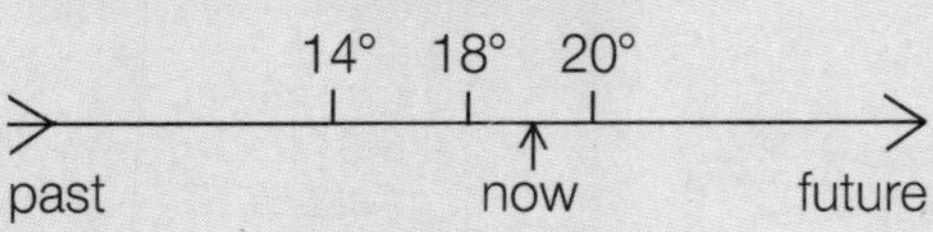

The leaves **are turning** brown.

4. Veränderungen während einer begrenzten Zeitspanne, die die Gegenwart einschließt.

You**'re** always **listening** to music.
(Das geht mir auf die Nerven)

Vergleiche:
You always **listen** to music, don't you?
(Du magst wohl gerne Musik?)
Jane **is** always **telling** funny stories.
(Das finde ich toll)
Jane always **tells** funny stories when I go to see her. (nur zu diesen Zeiten)

5. Gefühlsbetonte Beschreibungen von Gewohnheiten, häufig mit *always*.
   Der Sprecher drückt Verärgerung, Verwunderung oder Belustigung aus.

Und nun zu den Übungen.

Übung 1

Can you find the right pairs?

1. What are you doing?
2. What do you do for a living?
3. Would you like one?
4. Do you still smoke?
5. When do you have lunch?
6. Will you ring Diane for me?

a) No, thanks. I don't smoke.
b) I'm making a cupboard.
c) Yes, but later. She's just having lunch.
d) From twelve to one.
e) I make furniture.
f) Well, I'm just trying to stop.

Übung 2

This is Brenda relaxing at home. Look at the picture and write as much as you can about her. Use as many different verbs as you can.

§3 Statische Verben, normalerweise im simple present

Es gibt einige Verben, die im allgemeinen nur im ***simple present*** stehen. Sie drücken nämlich nicht einen Prozeß *(present continuous)*, sondern einen Zustand, eine Meinung, Einstellung oder Sinneswahrnehmung aus. Hierher gehören

1. Zustandsverben:

   a) Was jemand ist; der Anschein:
   be, look, seem, sound

   My father **is** a teacher.
   Those trousers **look** nice.
   The train **seems** to have left.
   That **sounds** like a fire-engine.

   b) Was jemand besitzt:
   belong, have (got), own

   That record **belongs** to me.

   c) Verben, die eine Beziehung ausdrücken:
   contain, depend on

   I don't know if I'm coming.
   It **depends on** the weather.

   d) Kosten, Maße:
   cost, measure, weigh

   How much **does** it **cost**?
   How much **do** you **weigh**?

2. Verben, die eine Meinung, Vermutung oder Wissen ausdrücken:
   agree, believe, forget, know, mean (meinen, bedeuten), *remember, suppose, think, understand*

   I **agree** with you.
   You **believe** me, don't you?
   Do you **know** what I mean?
   What **does** this word **mean**?

3. Verben, die eine gefühlsmäßige Einstellung ausdrücken:
   hate, hope, like, love, mind, need, prefer, want, wish

   My cat **hates** dogs.
   Do you **mind** if I open the window?
   Who **wants** an ice-cream?

4. Verben der Sinneswahrnehmung:
   see, hear, feel, taste, smell

   I **hear** you passed your exam.
   This fish **tastes** funny.

§4 Zustandsverben im simple present und im present continuous

Sie haben vielleicht schon bemerkt, daß einige dieser statischen Verben manchmal doch im ***present continuous*** erscheinen. Wie erklärt sich das?
Manche dieser Verben haben eine ganz andere Bedeutung, wenn sie in der ***continuous form*** erscheinen:

	simple present	**present continuous**
be	Sally **is** normally very sensible. (= sein)	Sally **is being** silly today. (= sich benehmen)
have	Brenda **has** two children. (= haben)	Karin **is having** a baby. (= schwanger sein)
see	You can **see** Dover from here. (= sehen)	Mrs Bailey **is** just **seeing** a customer. (= sich unterhalten, sich treffen)
think	I **don't think** you're right. (= glauben)	My brother **is thinking** of going to England next summer. (= planen)

Übung 3

Put the verbs in brackets into either the simple present or the present continuous. Do all the sentences before you look at the answers.

1. ..... you ..... to go and see a film?
   (want)
2. You ..... always ..... me to be quiet.
   (tell)
3. This plant looks as if it .....
   (die)
4. Marie's parents ..... not ..... her go to a disco.
   (let)
5. I ..... you have passed your exam. That's great.
   (hear)
6. Wendy's on the phone. She ..... she'll be here at seven.
   (say)
7. Andy ..... like his brother, doesn't he?
   (look)
8. My bike's broken down, so I ..... by bus this week.
   (travel)

9. What time ..... your mother usually ..... home from work?
   (get)
10. What's that noise? – It ..... like a helicopter.
   (sound)
11. I don't want any chips. I .....
   (slim)
12. My penfriend ..... from Wales.
   (come)
13. I've just read a fantastic book. It's about a woman who stole some jewelry from a shop. First she ..... to sell it, then she ..... out that the shop ..... to the mafia.
   (try, find, belong)
14. I don't know how to play this game. What ..... I .....?
   (do)
   – Watch me. First I .... the cards in front of me. Then I ..... one from the pile in the middle.
   (put, take)
15. ..... this dog ..... to you.
   (belong)

Before you look at the answers write down which rules helped you.

Wenn Sie meinen, Sie brauchen etwas mehr Übung, dann versuchen Sie den Abschnitt „Überprüfen Sie Ihr Wissen" noch einmal. Vielleicht schaffen Sie es diesmal ohne einen einzigen Fehler.

2. Simple past – present perfect

Sie wissen sicher aus Erfahrung, daß die richtige Anwendung des ***present perfect*** und ***simple past*** gar nicht so einfach ist. Aber keine Angst! Wenn Sie sich ein paar Regeln merken, ist es nicht so schwer.

Zunächst einige Beispiele für die zwei Formen:

present perfect	simple past
I **have been** at this school for five years.	I **was** at this school for five years.
Susan **has** just **kissed** me.	Susan **kissed** me last night.
Someone **has shot** the bank manager.	Someone **shot** the bank manager yesterday afternoon.
I **haven't had** lunch yet.	We **had** lunch an hour ago.
Have you **heard** the news?	I **heard** about the accident last night.
I **have seen** that film.	I **saw** that film last week.
Have you ever **been** in love?	I **was** in love twice last year.

Prüfen Sie jetzt bitte nach, inwieweit Sie diese zwei Zeitformen richtig anwenden können.

Überprüfen Sie Ihr Wissen

Test

Complete these sentences by putting the words in brackets into either the simple past or the present perfect.

1. Brian ..... a video recorder a few months ago. (buy)
2. I didn't know Brian had a video recorder –
   Yes, he ..... it for a few months now. (have)
3. Last year we ..... to Wales for our holidays. (go)
4. You're brown! – Yes, I ..... on holiday. (just be)
5. I can't come to the football match. I ..... my homework yet. (not do)
6. I ..... all my homework yesterday afternoon. (do)
7. Are you tired? – Yes, I ..... very well last night. (not sleep)
8. Are you tired? – Yes, I ..... a hard day. (have)
9. Here is the nine o'clock news: There ..... an accident on the M1 near Nottingham. (be)
10. I ..... my keys. (lose) – ..... you ..... them with you this morning? (take)
11. Where ..... you ..... at the weekend? (go)
12. Where ..... you .....? (be) You look very dirty.
13. ..... you ever ..... an accident? (have) – Yes, I ..... my leg skiing a few years ago. (break)
14. How long ..... you ..... your penfriend? (know) – Well, we ..... writing to each other about six months ago. (start)
15. My sister is going to Italy in the summer. That is why she ..... to learn Italian. (start)

Grammatikregeln und Übungen

§1 Gebrauch des simple past

I **went** to the cinema last night.

last night

Zeit des erzählten Vorgangs (ins Kino gehen)

Zeit des Sprechens

Das *simple past* bezieht sich auf eine bestimmte Zeit vor dem Zeitpunkt des Sprechens. Es wird vor allem in Erzählungen und Berichten verwendet.
Typische Zeitbestimmungen:
at two o'clock, an hour (three days ...) ago, yesterday afternoon, on Friday, last week, in 1985

§2 Gebrauch des present perfect

Man verwendet das ***present perfect*** in folgenden Fällen:

a) How long **have** you **been** here? (You are still here)
b) I **have known** John for years. (I still do)

Zeit des
a) Ankommens
b) Kennenlernens

Zeit des Sprechens

for three days
for years
for ages

1. Etwas hat in der Vergangenheit angefangen und dauert noch an. Die Zeit des Sprechens ist Teil dieser Zeitspanne.
Typische Zeitbestimmungen:
always, how long, for, since

!

I *have lived* here for years. –
Ich wohne schon seit Jahren hier.
We *have had* a dog since Christmas. –
Wir haben seit Weihnachten einen Hund.

for bezeichnet eine Zeitspanne

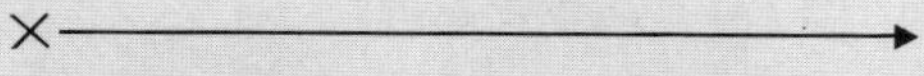

since Tuesday
since 1985
since we met

since bezeichnet den Ausgangspunkt einer Handlung oder eines Vorgangs

Would you like some tea?
– No, thanks. I**'ve just had** some.
You **have just won** a million pounds.

2. Etwas ist gerade eben geschehen.
Typische Zeitbestimmung:
just

Ann **has had** a baby.
(There is a baby in the family now)
Have you **had** a hard day?
(Are you tired?)
I **have seen** that film.
(I know what it is about)
Someone **has shot** the bank manager.
(He is dead)
I **have read** the newspaper.
(You can throw it away)

3. Wir interessieren uns mehr für das Ergebnis als für das, was geschehen ist. Aus dem Ergebnis können Folgerungen gezogen werden, oder es sind weitere Handlungen möglich.

I **have had** fish and chips several times.
Have you ever **been** in love?
Susan **hasn't kissed** me yet.

4. Etwas hat sich bis jetzt einmal, mehrmals oder nie ereignet.
Typische Zeitbestimmungen:
ever, never, often, several times, yet

!

Ever und *several times* werden oft mit „schon" und „schon mehrmals" übersetzt.

Have you **heard** the news?
Someone **broke** into Jean's flat.

Here are the main points of the news:
Princess Diana **has finished** her tour of Australia. She **arrived** home last night.
The number of unemployed **has risen**.
Another 2,000 jobs **were** lost.

5. Gespräche oder Berichte über vergangene Ereignisse werden im *present perfect* angefangen. Der genaue Zeitpunkt wird aber nicht erwähnt. Weitere Angaben (wann und wie es geschah, was darauf folgte usw.) stehen im *simple past*.

§3 Zeitadverbien im present perfect und im simple past

Oft kann man an den Zeitadverbien erkennen, welche Zeitform nötig ist,

z. B.: I have **just** had some tea. (§ 2.2)
Have you **ever** been in love? (§ 2.4)
I went to the cinema **last night.** (§ 1)

Manche Zeitadverbien können jedoch sowohl im ***present perfect*** als auch im ***simple past*** erscheinen. Es kommt auf die Einstellung des Sprechers zur Vergangenheit an:

I **haven't had** a cold this year.	Ich habe in diesem Jahr noch keinen Schnupfen gehabt. (Es kann noch kommen, weil das Jahr noch nicht vorbei ist.)
I **didn't have** a cold this year.	Ich hatte in diesem Jahr keinen Schnupfen. (Und ich werde wahrscheinlich keinen mehr bekommen, da das Jahr fast vorbei ist.)
Susan **has** never **kissed** me.	Bis jetzt hat Susan mich noch nicht geküßt.
Susan never **kissed** me.	Damals hat mich Susan nie geküßt. (Der Sprecher denkt an eine bestimmte Zeit in der Vergangenheit.)

! Im amerikanischen Englisch wird häufig das ***simple past*** verwendet, wo im britischen Englisch das ***present perfect*** erforderlich wäre:
AE: Did you find your key yet?
BE: Have you found your key yet?

You've overslept again, Henry

Übung 1

Warum wird in diesem Cartoon das ‚present perfect' und nicht das ‚simple past' gebraucht? Welche Regel ist ausschlaggebend?

Übung 2

What is the difference in meaning between these sentences?

1. I have been at this school for five years.
2. I was at this school for five years.
3. Alan has worked hard this morning.
4. Alan worked hard this morning.

In welchen der folgenden Sätze denkt der Sprecher an einen bestimmten Zeitpunkt? Was deutet darauf hin?

5. Did you go on holiday with friends?
6. I have often been away with friends.
7. My brother has never lent me any money.
8. My brother wouldn't lend me any money.
9. Did you eat all the cake?
10. Who has eaten all the cake?
11. Bus fares have gone up.
12. Bus fares went up a few weeks ago.

Welche Regeln treffen für den Gebrauch des ‚present perfect' in den Sätzen 1–12 zu?

No wonder we haven't had a single customer today – you forgot to unlock the doors.

Übung 3

Warum werden hier zwei verschiedene Zeiten benutzt?
Welche Regeln sind bei der Erklärung hilfreich?

Übung 4

Match up these two lists to make sentences. Use the simple past or the present perfect.

Example:

You – ride a horse? *ever* → *Have you ever ridden a horse?*

You – find your key?	Where
I – finish my homework	now
I – write four letters	since two o'clock
You – go on holiday?	last year
My parents – be abroad	never
You – live here now?	How long
You – like the film?	Why not
Your penfriend – answer your letter?	yet
I – hear the news	just
My mother – lend me her car	last night

Übung 5

A travel agency has advertised for a courier. The work involves taking tourists on guided coach tours of Europe for 2–6 weeks. They are looking for someone who can speak at least one foreign language, is confident and energetic and likes meeting people. Imagine you are the interviewer. Use the simple past or present perfect forms of the verbs.

Interviewer:	Now, Carol. What ..... your best subjects at school? (be)
Carol:	French and German.
Interviewer:	And you ..... school? (just – leave)
Carol:	Yes, I left at Easter.
Interviewer:	..... for any other jobs yet? (apply)
Carol:	Well, I've seen several advertised in the paper, but I haven't written yet.
Interviewer:	Who ..... you about this job? (tell)
Carol:	The job centre.
Interviewer:	And who ..... you ..... there? (talk to)
Carol:	Mrs Jenkins.
Interviewer:	I see. And when she ..... you why you ..... this job what ..... her? (ask – want – tell)
Carol:	I told her I've always wanted to travel and meet lots of people.
Interviewer:	I see. ...... ever ..... abroad? (be)
Carol:	Yes. Last summer I worked as an au pair in Paris.
Interviewer:	Alright, Carol. Thank you very much. Will you wait outside, please?

Interviewer:	Good morning, Mark. You're twenty minutes late. What .....? (happen)
Mark:	I'm afraid I missed the bus.
Interviewer:	..... late? (get up)
Mark:	No, but my mother didn't feel well, so I had to get breakfast for my little sister.
Interviewer:	I see. So that's why you ..... time to clean your shoes before you came out. (not have) Now, Mark, you ..... several jobs since you ..... school. Why? ..... them? (have – leave – not like)
Mark:	No, not really. I wanted something more interesting.
Interviewer:	..... any foreign languages at school? (learn)
Mark:	Yes, French and Spanish.
Interviewer:	And ..... ever ..... those countries? (visit)
Mark:	Oh yes. Last summer I went camping in Spain and the year before I worked on a farm in France for six months.
Interviewer:	Alright, Mark. Thank you. Wait outside for a moment please.

Who would you give the job to and why?

Underline all the words which helped you to choose the present perfect.

3. Past continuous – simple past

Sind Sie manchmal unsicher, wann ***past continuous*** und wann ***simple past*** zu verwenden ist? Dieses Kapitel wird Ihnen helfen, diese zwei Formen auseinanderzuhalten. Zuerst einige Beispiele:

past continuous	**past continuous/simple past**
What **were** you **doing** at about seven last night? I **was thinking** of going to town this afternoon. I **was going** to stay in tonight.	Jimmy **was dancing** on the table when the teacher **came in.** Sherlock Holmes **was sitting** in his armchair. He **was reading** a newspaper. Suddenly he **heard** footsteps.

Überprüfen Sie Ihr Wissen

Test

Put the verbs in brackets into the simple past or past continuous.

1. It ..... dark when we finally ..... home. (get, get)
2. Have you seen my gloves? I ..... them when I ..... (wear, arrive)
3. 'What are you doing this afternoon?' – 'I ..... of trying out my new camera. Do you want to help me?' (think)
4. This time last week we ..... still ..... our holiday. (enjoy)
5. We ..... our holiday very much. We went to Cornwall. (enjoy)
6. When the postman ...... the bell I ..... a shower. (ring, have)
7. 'Have you any plans for Saturday night?' 'Not really. I ..... to stay in.' (go)
8. I ..... the phone because I ..... to a record. (not hear, listen)
9. All the time that woman ..... I ..... of something else. (talk, think)
10. I ..... if you could give me a lift into town? (wonder)
11. Mike said he ..... to talk because he ..... the next train. (not be able to stop, catch)
12. Mike ..... to talk for a minute before he ..... his train. (stop, catch)
13. Who ..... when the accident .....? (drive, happen)
14. As soon as I ..... your letter I quickly ..... my breakfast, ... my coat, ... to the bus stop and here I am. (get, finish, grab, run)
15. Aunt Catherine ..... to see us tonight, but she can't come now because her car won't start. (come)

Grammatikregeln und Übungen

§1 Gebrauch des past continuous

Man verwendet das ***past continuous*** in folgenden Fällen:

What **were** you **doing** at about seven last night?

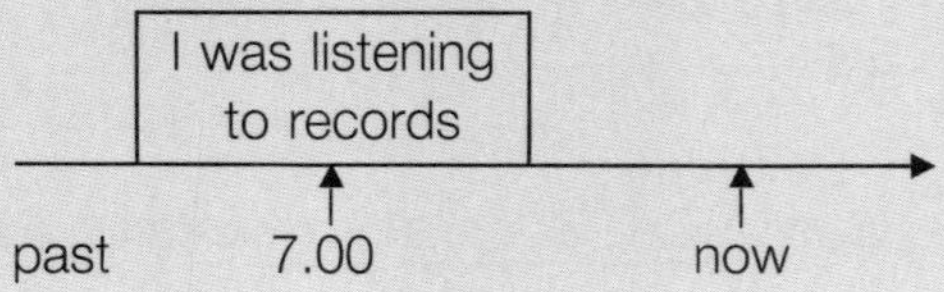

1. Um auszudrücken, daß eine Handlung zu einem bestimmten Zeitpunkt in der Vergangenheit gerade vor sich ging, d. h. noch nicht zu Ende war.

'What are you doing this afternoon?' 'I **was thinking** of going to town.' („Aber wenn Du einen anderen Vorschlag hast, bin ich einverstanden.")

I **was thinking** of going to town this afternoon. („Willst Du mitgehen?")

I **was wondering** if you could lend me five pounds?

2. Um höflich zu sein:
   a) wenn man anderen den Eindruck geben will, daß ihre Ideen wichtiger sind als die eigenen,
   b) wenn man andere indirekt einladen will,
   c) wenn man um etwas bitten will.

My girlfriend **was coming** to the party, but unfortunately she's ill.
I **was going** to stay in tonight, but I've changed my mind.

3. Um eine Meinungs- oder Umstandsänderung auszudrücken; es war etwas beabsichtigt, was jedoch nicht eingetreten ist.
   Häufige Verben: *come, go, expect, intend, look forward to, plan, arrange*

At the station we met some friends who **were travelling** to Edinburgh.

4. Um über einen Vorgang zu sprechen, der zu einem bestimmten Zeitpunkt in der Vergangenheit noch nicht angefangen hatte, aber sicher eintreten würde.

§2 Past continuous und simple past im Vergleich

Jimmy **was dancing** on the table (1) when the teacher came in (2).

I **was doing** my homework (1) when Sue came in and kissed me. (2)

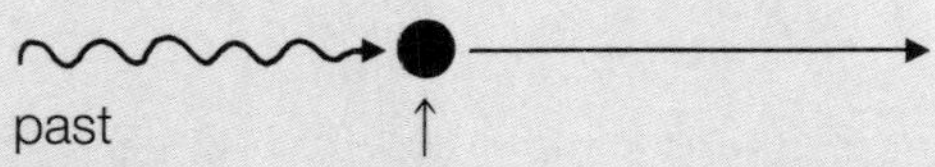

1. Das *past continuous* beschreibt, was zu einem bestimmten Zeitpunkt in der Vergangenheit gerade vorging, also die Hintergrundshandlung (1), als ein neues Ereignis (2) eintrat. Für das neue Ereignis verwendet man das *simple past*.

!

Einige Verben kommen normalerweise nicht in der Verlaufsform vor (vgl. Kap. ‚Simple present – present continous' §3).

Ann **was trying** to do her homework, while her father **was watching** television.

Ken **came** into the room, **threw** his bag on the floor and **said**, "I've decided to become a pop star."

2. Wenn mehrere Vorgänge gleichzeitig im Ablauf waren, so steht in allen Fällen das *past continuous*.

(Um auszudrücken, daß mehrere abgeschlossene Vorgänge aufeinanderfolgten, benutzt man dagegen das *simple past*.

Sherlock Holmes **was sitting** in his favourite armchair. He **was reading** a newspaper and **smoking** his favourite pipe. (Hintergrundshandlungen).
Suddenly he **heard** footsteps outside his door. (Neues, abgeschlossenes Ereignis).

3. Das *past continuous* wird häufig für beschreibende Teile in Erzählungen oder Berichten benutzt, d. h. zur Beschreibung von Hintergrundshandlungen oder Begleitumständen.

Übung 1

Use the past continuous or simple past forms of the verbs in brackets to find out the story of the stolen jewels.

Lord and Lady Richmouth . . . . . (give) another of their famous parties. As usual, there were hundreds of guests. They . . . . . all . . . . . (wear) their most expensive clothes and jewelry. Everyone . . . . . (have) a wonderful time. A band . . . . . (play) and some people . . . . . (dance). Others . . . . . (stand) around in small groups, ... (talk) and . . . . . (laugh). Almost everyone . . . . . (eat) or . . . . . (drink) something.

Suddenly Sally Starlight, the famous film star, ... (scream): "Someone's stolen my necklace! Help!"

A few minutes later the Inspector . . . . . (arrive). She . . . . . (interview) all the guests in turn:

Inspector:	Now, Miss Gaygirl, what . . . . . you . . . . . (do) when Miss Starlight noticed that her necklace had been stolen?
Miss G.:	I . . . . . (talk) to General Blimp, wasn't I, General?
General:	That's right, my dear. You . . . . . (tell) me about your new horses.
Inspector:	And what about you, Mr Steel? What . . . . . you . . . . . (do)?
Mr Steel:	I . . . . . (dance) with Mrs Heavyfoot. I danced with her all night, without stopping.
Inspector:	Is that right, Mrs Heavyfoot?
Mrs H.:	Well, yes. That is – no, not quite. Just before Miss Starlight cried out he left the room.
Inspector:	What? Hey, come back! He's running away.

Übung 2

Put these two lists together. Explain the difference between each pair of sentences.

1. a) When I got to the party
   b) When I got to the party

2. a) What were you doing when the lights went out?
   b) What did you do when the lights went out?

3. a) The girl was drowning . . . . .
   b) The girl drowned . . . . .

4. a) When the phone rang . . . . .
   b) When the phone rang . . . . .

5. a) When I looked at the baby . . . . .
   b) When I looked at the baby . . . . .

6. a) What did you do when your brother fell into the river?
   b) What were you doing when your brother fell into the river?

- I lit a candle.
- I got out of the shower and answered it.
- I was having a shower, so I couldn't answer it.
- it was crying.
- I jumped in after him.
- it cried.
- I was having a shower.
- I was just a few metres away, fishing.
- everyone went home.
- They couldn't save her.
- everyone was going home.
- but they saved her.

Übung 3

Use the past continuous or simple past forms of the verbs in brackets to complete these sentences.

1. At nine o'clock we ..... still ..... for Tony. (wait)
2. When we finally ..... at the station the train ..... just ..... (arrive, leave)
3. 'Are you doing anything at the weekend?' 'Well, I ..... to go to the football match, but if you want to do anything else I don't mind.' (plan)
4. Who ..... you ..... to when I ..... you yesterday? (talk, see)
5. We ..... the cathedral because it ..... (not be able to visit, repair)
6. This time last year we ...... exams. (do)
7. We ..... of going to the disco. Would you like to come? (think)
8. '..... Johnny last night? He ..... black tights and a fur coat.' (you see, wear)
9. When it ..... to rain everyone who ..... the match ..... up an umbrella. (start, watch, put)
10. 'I thought you ..... out tonight?' 'I was, but my bike won't start.' (go)
11. When Judy ..... the burglar she ..... the door, ... into the cellar and ..... a hammer. (hear, lock, run, fetch)
12. While Kevin ..... in England he ..... a very nice girl. (stay, meet)
13. My car won't start. I ..... if you could give me a hand? (wonder)

Übung 4

Use the past continuous and simple past forms once each to complete each pair of sentences.

<u>Example:</u>

Sally – listen to the news – while – have a bath
Sally listened to the news while she was having a bath

Sally – listen to the news – then – have a bath
Sally listened to the news, then she had a bath.

1. a) When – the teacher – walk in – pupils – listen to music and dance.
   b) When – the teacher – walk in – pupils – stop dancing.
2. a) Linda – go home by taxi – miss – last bus.
   b) John – go home by taxi – rain so hard.
3. a) I – not hear the announcement – somebody – talk
   b) I – not hear the announcement – somebody – switch the radio off

Übung 5

Write the story, using the past continuous and simple past. Find your own ending.

You chaps seen any reindeers pass this way?

One day Santa Claus – not find – reindeers. So – go out – look for. It – snow. Suddenly – meet two men. They – sit next to a fire. On the fire – saucepan – food in it. The men – eat some meat. The meat – look like Santa's reindeers. When Santa – see what the men – eat he .....

4. Present perfect continuous – present perfect simple form – past perfect

Die richtige Anwendung des ***present perfect continuous*** ist nicht ganz einfach. Aber keine Angst!
Wenn sie dieses Kapitel durchgearbeitet haben, werden Sie hoffentlich keine Fehler mehr machen.

Zunächst einige Beispiele:

present perfect simple	present perfect continuous
I **have** never **danced** with Keith.	We **have been dancing** all night.
Tina **has told** me about her holidays.	Tina **has been talking** for hours.
Julie **has painted** a picture.	Julie **has been painting** all day.
Someone **has eaten** my biscuits.	Someone **has been eating** my biscuits.
I've cleaned the whole flat.	**I've been cleaning** all morning.
Have you **played** tennis before?	How long **have** you **been playing** tennis?
Angela **has learnt** to ski.	Angela **has been learning** to ski for years.
Which countries **have** you **lived** in?	**I've been living** in America since 1986.

past perfect
Kevin didn't go to the cinema with us because he **had seen** the film before. If you **had asked** me I would have lent you some money.

Prüfen Sie nach, ob Sie diese Formen richtig anwenden können.

Überprüfen Sie Ihr Wissen

Test 1

Complete these sentences by using the simple or continuous forms of the present perfect.

1. I ..... my homework. (do) Now I can go out.
2. I ..... my homework for three hours. (do)
3. 'What ..... you ..... all afternoon?' (do) 'I ..... that book you lent me (read), but I ..... it yet. (not finish)
4. Esmeralda is a famous film star. She ..... films since she was sixteen. She ..... about ten films. (make, make)
5. How long ..... Jill ..... (go) out with Ron?
6. How long ..... Jill and Ron ..... each other? (know)
7. Sue ..... to ring you all morning. (try)
8. Sue ..... to ring you several times. (try)
9. I ..... always ..... English. (like)

Test 2

These sentences are all wrong. They are typical mistakes made by Germans. Can you correct them?

1. It is raining all day.
2. How long are you waiting for me?
3. I am knowing my girlfriend for three months.
4. Julie has painted all day.
5. How long do you learn English? You're very good.
6. Your eyes are red. Have you cried?
7. I'm tired. I've worked very hard today.
8. Sally has been having a cold for ages.
9. We have been living here since two years.

Grammatikregeln und Übungen

§ 1 Gebrauch des present perfect continuous

Das ***present perfect continuous*** wird verwendet:

David **has been skiing** since he was five.

1. Für länger andauernde Situationen oder Handlungen, die in der Vergangenheit angefangen haben und bis in die Gegenwart andauern. Der Vorgang kann auch unterbrochen gewesen sein.
   Häufige Zeitbestimmungen, mit denen man angibt oder fragt, wie lange die Situation schon andauert:
   all (day), the whole (afternoon), how long, for, since

   (Für den Unterschied zwischen *for* und *since* siehe Kap. ,*Present perfect – simple past*‘ §2.1)

Tina **has** just **been telling** me about her holidays.

2. Für länger andauernde Situationen und Vorgänge, die gerade zu Ende gegangen sind.
   Verben, bei denen das *present perfect continuous* häufig gebraucht wird:
   live, learn, study, sit, stand, talk, tell, wait, walk (d. h. Verben, die länger andauernde Vorgänge ausdrücken können)

Tina **has been talking** about her holidays all afternoon.	**!** a) Um die Dauer eines Vorgangs oder einer Situation auszudrücken, gebraucht man das *present perfect continuous*, nicht das *present continuous.*
I **have loved** Eric for years.	b) Es gibt Verben, die normalerweise keine *continuous form* bilden, z. B. *like, hate, love, see, hear, know, remember, wish, be, belong* (vgl. Kap. ‚*Simple present – present continuous*', §3).

Das ***present continuous*** *(I am doing)* wird oft fälschlicherweise anstelle des ***present perfect continuous*** *(I have been doing)* verwendet. Die nächste Übung hilft Ihnen, diesen Fehler zu vermeiden.

Übung 1

Translate the following sentences, using the present continuous or present perfect continuous.

1. Es regnet.
2. Es regnet schon seit heute morgen.
3. Mr Williams redet schon eine Stunde lang.
4. Mr Williams redet über seine Operation.
5. Meine Freundin lernt Italienisch.
6. Seit sechs Monaten lernt meine Freundin Italienisch.

Look at the English translations. Which two words show you when you need the present perfect continuous form?

Übung 2

Complete each sentence in two different ways, using 'for' and 'since'. The following words will help you: (two) o'clock, (three) hours, half an hour, ten minutes, six months, breakfast, (he) came home (from school), March .....

1. Dad ..... (make) dinner	since .....
	for .....
2. Grandad ..... (sing)	since .....
	for .....
3. My boyfriend ..... (work) on his computer	since .....
	for .....
4. Kevin ..... (look) for a job	since .....
	for .....

§2 Present perfect simple und present perfect continuous im Vergleich

present perfect, simple form	**present perfect, continuous form**
 Julie **has painted** a picture	 Julie **has been painting.**
1. Die Tätigkeit ist schon beendet, hatte aber ein Ergebnis, für das wir uns interessieren. I **have read** that book you lent me. (Now I know what it is about.) Someone **has eaten** my biscuits. (There aren't any left.)	1. Wir interessieren uns für die Tätigkeit. Es ist unwichtig, ob der Vorgang schon zu Ende ist oder nicht. I **have been reading** that book you lent me. Someone **has been eating** my biscuits. (There may be some left, or not.)
I**'ve cleaned** the whole flat. (The flat is clean.) Tony **has** just **run** all the way home from school. (Now he is hot.)	2. Die Tätigkeit hatte eine Folge. Wir interessieren uns eher dafür, wie es zu dieser Folge kam als für die Folge selber. I'm tired. **I've been cleaning** all day. (That is why I'm tired.) Tony is hot. He **has** just **been running.** (That is why he is hot.)
2. Etwas hat sich bis jetzt einmal, mehrmals oder nie ereignet ('ever, often, never ...). I **have often danced** with Keith. Sally **has played** table tennis **hundreds of times.**	3. Das *present perfect continuous* wird verwendet, wenn man sich eher für die Dauer eines Vorgangs interessiert. Keith **has been dancing all evening.** Sally **has been playing** table tennis **since she could walk.** **!** Die deutschen Entsprechungen des *present perfect continuous:* What *have* you *been doing* lately? (= Was hast Du in der letzten Zeit gemacht?) I *have been waiting* for ages. (= Ich warte schon ewig.)

Übung 3

Read the situation, then write two sentences, one with the simple and one with the continuous form of the present perfect.

Example:

Karin collects stamps. She started collecting them two years ago.

(She/collect stamps/two years) — *She has been collecting stamps for two years.*

(She/collect/about two thousand) — *She has collected about two thousand.*

1. Don can drive a car. He took the test six months ago.
   (He/drive/six months) .....
   (He/drive/about five thousand kilometres) .....
2. 'You look slimmer than the last time I saw you.'
   (Yes, I/slim) '.....'
   (Yes, I/lose/a lot of weight) '.....'
3. 'Have you been helping Alan with his homework?'
   (Yes, I/explain something to him)' '.....'
   (Oh, I/explain it so often/but/still can't do it) '.....'

Which rules helped you to answer these questions?

Übung 4

Imagine you are talking to some friends. Ask questions with 'How long', 'How many' and 'How often'. Use the simple or continuous forms of the present perfect.

Example:

Your friend is learning French.	*How long have you been learning French?*
1. Your friend is waiting for you.	...............................?
2. Your friend collects stamps.	How long ....?
	How many ....?
3. Trevor is on holiday	....................? (be on holiday)
4. Your friend is smoking.	How long ....?
	How many .... today?
5. Your friend has a cold.	...............................?
6. Your friend has borrowed one of your books without asking.	.... before you borrow anything? (tell you to ask me)

‚How long' ist ein Signalwort für das .....
Ausnahmen: Verben, wie ..... (Frage .....), ... (Frage .....), ..., die normalerweise keine ..... bilden. (Vgl. § .....).

Übung 5

Can you match up these lists?

1. I have had six cups of tea already.
2. I have been drinking tea all day.
3. Charlie has drunk eight pints of beer.
4. Charlie has been drinking.
5. I have been walking to school all week.
6. I have often walked to school.
7. Dennis has been spending a lot of money lately.
8. Dennis has spent a lot of money on his motor bike.

The buses were on strike.
I wonder where he got it from?
Haven't you?
And your mother has just poured me a seventh.
Have you seen it?
Now he can't stand up.
There was nothing else to do.
I could never drink so many.

§3 Present perfect continuous und simple past im Vergleich

present perfect continuous	**simple past**
David **has been skiing** since he was five.	**When did** he **start** skiing? He **started when he was five.**
Angela **has been playing** the guitar **for** years.	Angela **learnt** to play the guitar **years ago.**
How long has Sheila **been going** out with Tom?	Sheila **asked** Tom to go out with her about **two weeks ago.**
Wenn man sich eher dafür interessiert, wie lange eine Situation oder ein Vorgang schon andauert, benutzt man das *present perfect continuous*. Häufige Zeitbestimmungen: *how long, for, since.*	Wenn man sagen oder fragen will, wann etwas passiert ist, benutzt man das *simple past.*

Übung 6

Ask questions with 'how long' and 'when'.

1. Lynne is learning judo.
   (How long/she/learn judo?) .....
   (When/she/start learning judo?) .....

2. Marion is waiting for Dennis.
   (How long/she/wait?) .....
   (When/she/arrive?) .....

3. Mike is working in Glasgow
   (How long/he/work there?) .....
   (When/he/leave Wales?) .....

Übung 7

Mr Gambol has hurt his finger.
Mrs Gambol: (How/you/do it?) .....
Mr Gambol: (use/my pocket calculator/all day) .....

§4 Simple past, present perfect simple und continuous form im Überblick

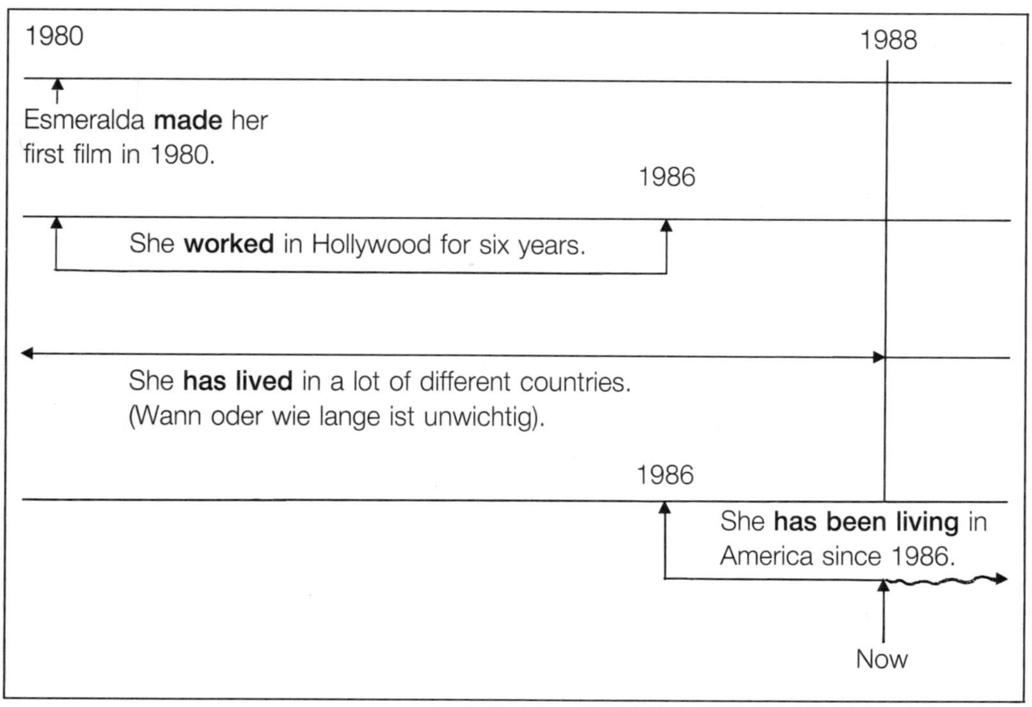

Übung 8

It is Saturday. Mike doesn't go to work on Saturdays, but he does a lot of other things. Today he was very busy.

From 9.00 to 10.00 he cleaned his flat.
At 10.00 he did some washing.
At 10.30 he made a cake.
At 11.00 he started to paint a cupboard.
From 11.45 to 12.15 he practised the guitar.
At 12.15 he had lunch.

After lunch he read the paper, then washed the pots.
From 13.30 to 14.00 he wrote some letters.
From 14.00 to 15.00 he played table tennis.
From 15.30 to 16.00 he put his holiday photos into an album.
At 16.00 he started doing the ironing.
At 17.00 he had tea.
At 18.00 he fell asleep.
Now it's 20.00. He was so tired he's still asleep!

Can you talk about what Mike did today?

Example:
It's 10.00. Mike has cleaned his flat. He started at nine and he's been cleaning for an hour.

It's 10.30. Mike ..... some washing. He ..... at 10.00 and he ..... it ..... half an hour.
It's 11.10. Mike ..... a cake and he ..... to ..... a cupboard. He .... it since 11.00.
It's 12.15. Mike ..... to ..... half an hour ago. He has .... 11.45.
It's 14.00. Mike ..... his lunch. After that he ..... the pots. He ..... letters ..... half an hour.
It's 14.45. Mike has .... 14.00.
It's 16.30. Mike ..... his holiday photos into an album. Now he ..... the ironing. He ..... half an hour.
Now it's 19.00. Mike ..... his tea and ..... asleep. He ..... asleep ..... 18.00.

§5 Gebrauch des past perfect

Das ***past perfect*** wird verwendet für:

Jeff **had** already **bought** the tickets when Sue said she wasn't going. Kevin didn't go to the cinema with us because he **had seen** the film before. When I arrived at the party most people **had left.** (Vgl.: When I arrived most people **left!**)	1. Ein Geschehen, das vor einem bestimmten Zeitpunkt in der Vergangenheit stattgefunden hat.
I was very surprised. I **hadn't seen** a camel before.	2. Einen Zustand, der vor einem bestimmten Zeitpunkt in der Vergangenheit begann und zu diesem Zeitpunkt noch andauerte.
How long **had** you **been waiting** when your boyfriend finally arrived? We **had** only **been talking** for a few minutes when my bus came.	3. Wenn eine Handlung oder ein Zustand bis zu einem Zeitpunkt der Vergangenheit noch andauerte und Ablauf oder Dauer besonders betont werden sollen, wird die *progressive form* gebraucht.
Jane phoned all her friends to tell them that she **had passed** her exams.	4. Das *past perfect* wird oft in der indirekten Rede verwendet. (Vgl. Kap. ‚Indirect speech', §4.2)
If you **had asked** me I would have lent you some money. I **wish** I **had worked** harder for the exams.	5. Nach *if, if only* und *wish* drückt das *past perfect* aus, daß etwas nicht eingetreten ist. (Vgl. Kap. ‚If-clauses', §5)

5. Future time

Im Englischen gibt es viele Möglichkeiten, über die Zukunft zu reden. Die Wahl der richtigen Form hängt davon ab, was man ausdrücken will. Hier zunächst eine Übersicht über die Zukunftsformen:

We **won't be** back before tea	**will-future**
That plane **is going to** crash.	**going to-future**
Dorothy **is working** next Saturday	**present continuous-future**
What time **does** the film **start?**	**simple present-future**
I'll ring you when I **get** home	**simple present-future after 'if, when ...'**
I'll be playing football between four and five.	**future continuous**
The concert **won't have finished** by nine.	**future perfect**
By six o' clock Sue **will have been dancing** for 48 hours.	**future perfect continuous**

Das sieht zunächst vielleicht etwas verwirrend aus. Aber nur keine Angst! Prüfen Sie erst einmal nach, was Sie schon können.

Überprüfen Sie Ihr Wissen

Test

Choose the correct future forms to complete these sentences.

1. 'Can you come tomorrow night?' 'Sorry, I ..... table tennis.
   (play/will play/am playing)
2. What time ..... the concert .....?
   (does ..... end/will ..... end)
3. If you ...... here by seven I'll leave without you.
   (aren't/won't be)
4. The sun is coming out. It ..... be a nice day.
   (is going to/will)
5. Do you think the world ..... a better place in 100 years time?
   (is/will be)
6. 'I can't open this tin.' 'I ..... do it for you'.
   (am going to/will)
7. What do you want to do when you ..... school?
   (leave/will leave)
8. Diana ..... work with computers.
   (is going to/will)
9. Don't come before five. I ..... my homework.
   (will do/will be doing)
10. By this time next week I ..... all my exams.
    (will finish/will have finished)
11. By ten o'clock I ..... for four hours.
    (will have worked/will have been working)

Grammatikregeln und Übungen

§1 Übersicht über die verschiedenen Futurformen

will	– künftiges Geschehen, das der Sprecher nicht beeinflussen kann – Vermutungen und Voraussagen – spontane Entschlüsse und Versprechen	It **will** soon **be** dark. We **won't be** back before tea. **I'll help** you.	§2.1 §2.2 §2.3
going to	– fester Vorsatz – Schlußfolgerungen aus der Gegenwart	Jill **is going to** be an engineer. That plane **is going to** crash.	§3.1 §3.2
present continuous	fest beschlossener, vereinbarter Plan, meist mit Zeitangabe	Dorothy **is working** on Saturday.	§4
simple present	– künftiges Geschehen als Teil eines Fahrplans oder festgelegten Programms – Bedingungen nach *if, when*	What time **does** the film **start?** I'll ring you when I **get** home.	§5.1 §5.2
future continuous	– Vorgang, der zu einem bestimmten Zeitpunkt in der Zukunft (noch) abläuft – üblicherweise eintretendes Geschehen – Erkundigungen, ohne neugierig oder aufdringlich zu wirken	Don't ring between 4 and 5. **I'll be playing** football. **I'll be passing** the letter box anyway. **Will** you **be paying** cash?	§6.1 §6.2 §6.3
future perfect **future perfect continuous**	Aussagen oder Erkundigungen darüber, ob ein Vorgang zu einem bestimmten Zeitpunkt in der Zukunft abgeschlossen sein wird oder nicht, immer mit Zeitbestimmung Vorgang, der zu einem bestimmten Zeitpunkt in der Zukunft schon seit einiger Zeit andauert, von der Zukunft aus gesehen	The concert **won't have finished** by nine. By six o'clock Sue **will have been dancing** for 48 hours.	§7.1 §7.2

§2 Das will-future

Manchmal wird *shall* anstatt *will* verwendet, aber nur mit *I* oder *we*.

We **shall/will** probably have a class party next week.
I **shan't/won't** be here tomorrow.

Will ist häufiger als *shall*. *Shall* wird vorwiegend für Vorschläge und Angebote benutzt:

Shall I open the window?
Where **shall** we go tonight?

Im gesprochenen Englisch hört man in Aussagesätzen meistens nur die Kurzform ***'ll***

Das ***will-future*** wird verwendet für:

It **will** soon **be** dark.
I**'ll be** eighteen next year.

1. Künftiges Geschehen, das der Sprecher nicht beeinflussen kann.

Do you **think** Carol **will get** the job?
My father **won't like** my new hairstyle.
We **probably won't be** back before ten.

I **expect** we**'ll find** the way.

2. Vermutungen und Voraussagen, oft nach *be sure, expect, imagine, suppose, think, perhaps, probably.*

   Im Deutschen ist es meist unwichtig, ob man das Präsens (wir finden den Weg) oder das Futur (wir werden den Weg finden) benutzt. Im Englischen muß man in solchen Fällen das *will-future* verwenden (nicht das *simple present*).

I**'ll meet** you in half an hour.
I**'ll help** you with your homework.
I **won't be** long.

3. Spontane Entschlüsse und Versprechen. Hier steht im Deutschen meist die Gegenwart (Wir treffen uns ...).

!

I will = **ich werde**
ich will = **I want**

§3 Das going to-future

Wir verwenden ***going to*** für:

What **are** you **going to** do when you leave school? Jill **is going to** be an engineer.	1. Künftige Ereignisse, über die wir uns vorher bereits Gedanken gemacht haben und zu einem festen Entschluß gekommen sind.
Marion **is going to** have a baby. Look at that plane. It**'s going to** land.	2. Schlußfolgerungen aus einem gegenwärtigen Zustand.

! Bei den Verben ***go*** und ***come*** wird aus stilistischen Gründen normalerweise keine ***going to*** Form gebraucht. Statt dessen steht das ***present continuous***:
We're going on holiday in July. (nicht *‚going to go'*)
Are you coming to the party tonight? (nicht *‚going to come'*)

Übung 1

1. Jenny has just written a letter, but she can't find an envelope.
   Jenny: Linda, we haven't got any envelopes, have we?
   Linda: No, but I'm just going out. I'll get some.
   Before she goes she talks to Carol.
   Linda: I'm going to get some envelopes. Can I get you anything, Carol?

In welchem Satz
a) wird der Entschluß erst im Moment des Sprechens gefaßt?
b) wurde der Entschluß vor dem Moment des Sprechens gefaßt?

Überlegen Sie bei den folgenden Sätzen, ob eine spontane Äußerung oder ein fester Entschluß vorliegt, und vervollständigen Sie dann bitte die Sätze.

2. Diane : My car won't start. I'll be late for work.
   Sue : Don't worry. I ..... take you.
   A few minutes later Sue talks to her husband.
   Sue : I ..... take Diane to work. Her car won't start.
3. Helen : Can you mend my bike, Dad?
   Father : Alright, but not just now. I ..... do it later.
4. Mrs Smith : Bill, has Helen told you about her bike?
   Mr Smith Yes, I ..... do it later.
5. John : Are you going shopping?
   Alan : Yes, I ..... buy something for tea.
6. Dave : I don't know how to use this camera.
   Janet : It's easy. I ..... show you.

Übung 2

Fill in 'will' or 'going to' and say which rule helped you.

1. Kevin hasn't done any work for his exam. He ..... fail.
2. 'Do you think you ..... pass the exam?' 'I don't know, but I ..... try very hard.'
3. 'What would you like to drink?' 'I ..... have a coffee, please.'
4. You'd better put your coat on. It ..... be cold.
5. 'Where ..... spend your holidays this year?' 'I expect we ..... go to France, as usual.'
6. Look at that stupid driver. There's ..... be an accident.
7. Oh no! I've no money left. I ..... have to walk home.
8. I'm sure Bob ..... come if you ask him.
9. When ..... invite Bob to your party?
10. Soon there ..... be many wild animals left on the earth.

Wenn Sie glauben, den Unterschied zwischen *will* und *going to* verstanden zu haben, fahren Sie bitte im Text fort. Wenn nicht, lesen Sie die Regeln bitte noch einmal durch.

§4 Das present continuous-future

Das ***present continuous*** kann auch benutzt werden, um über die Zukunft zu sprechen:

Dorothy **is working** on Saturday. What time **are** you **meeting** Jill?	Das *present continuous* drückt einen fest beschlossenen, vereinbarten Plan aus, meist mit Zeitangabe.

Prüfen Sie, ob Ihnen der Unterschied zwischen *going to* und dem *present continuous* klar ist.

Übung 3

Cross out the wrong forms and say why.

1. It is raining/going to rain tomorrow.
2. You're falling/going to fall if you're not careful.

Übung 4

Which of these sentences makes the better excuse? Why?

1. I can't come on Saturday. I'm meeting Jill.
2. I can't come on Saturday. I'm going to meet Jill.

§5 Das simple present-future

Das ***simple present*** mit futurischer Bedeutung wird benutzt für:

What time **does** the film **start**?
The school holidays **begin** next Thursday.
Tomorrow **is** Wednesday.

1. Zukünftiges Geschehen, das durch Termine, Fahrplan, Programm usw. bereits festgelegt ist; häufig bei Verben wie *begin, start, end, open, close, leave, arrive*.

Will your parents be angry **if** you**'re** late?
I'll ring you **when** I **get** home.
Think carefully **before** you **answer** this question.
If it **rains** we'll go by bus.
(Im Deutschen würde man die Gegenwart benutzen:
Wenn es **regnet, fahren** wir mit dem Bus).

2. Bedingungen, die mit *if* eingeleitet werden; in Nebensätzen nach *when, before, until, till, as soon as.*

!

if = wenn (etwas wird vielleicht geschehen)
when = wenn, als (etwas wird bestimmt geschehen)

!

I'll come when **I've finished**. (nicht *'will have finished'.)

Übung 5

Finish each sentence so that it means the same as the one before.

Example:
The journey takes two hours.
If you leave at five you will arrive at seven.

1. People who eat too much get fat.
   If you ..... too much you ..... fat.
2. Careful drivers do not have accidents.
   If you ..... carefully you ..... an accident.
3. There are lots of interesting things to see in London.
   You ..... lots of interesting things when you ..... to London.
4. Orders only take a few days.
   If you ..... the record it ..... here in a few days.

Übung 6

Put in 'if' or 'when'. Check rule §5.2. again first.

1. Ben might phone. ..... he does, tell him I'll ring back.
2. We'll go by bus ..... you don't want to walk.
3. Shall we go for a coffee ..... we've finished?
4. Margaret will notice a lot of changes ..... she gets home.
5. ..... we're not there by ten don't wait.
6. What are you going to be ..... you grow up?

Übung 7

Fill in 'if' or 'when' to find out what the cartoon says.
Which rule explains why the man uses the future form 'going to'?

And tell him ..... he does it again
I'm going to keep it!

Übung 8

Put the verbs into the simple present or present continuous future forms.

1. The pop concert ..... (start) at half past seven.
2. Jenny ..... (have) a party next Saturday.
3. Tony, we ..... (go) to the disco. ..... (you/come) with us?
4. What time ..... (your friend/come)?
5. What time ..... (the bus/leave)?

§6 Das future continuous

Das ***future continuous*** wird verwendet für:

Don't come between 5 and 6.
We**'ll be having** tea.

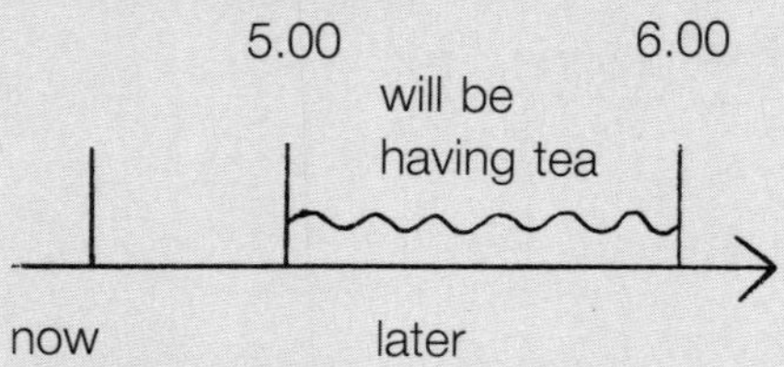

I wonder if it **will** still **be raining** this afternoon.

1. Vorgänge von begrenzter Dauer, die zu einem bestimmten Zeitpunkt in der Zukunft (noch) im Verlauf sind.

!

When I get home I'll have tea.

I'll have tea erfolgt nach dem Heimkommen.

I'll post that letter for you.
I'll be passing the letter box anyway.
The shops **will be closing** in half an hour.

2. Vorgänge, die üblicherweise eintreten, ohne besonders geplant zu sein, häufig mit *anyway.*

Will you **be seeing** Tony when you go to Wales?
Will you **be paying** cash or by cheque?

3. Erkundigungen nach einem Vorhaben klingen nicht so neugierig oder aufdringlich, wenn sie im *future continuous* ausgedrückt werden.

So viele Möglichkeiten, über die Zukunft zu reden! Prüfen Sie nach, ob Sie auch diese neue Möglichkeit richtig nutzen können.

Übung 9

Make sentences with 'will be ..... ing'!

1. I'm going to a computer programming course tonight. It starts at 7.30 and ends at 10.00. So from 7.30 to 10.00 I ..... (learn) to program computers.
2. My piano lesson is from 4 till 5. So at half past four I ..... (play) the piano.
3. My homework will take at least three hours. It's five o'clock now, so at seven I ..... (still/ work).

Which rule explains why we use the future continuous in these sentences?

Übung 10

Steve: I have to go to town tomorrow afternoon, but there's something wrong with my bike. And it's so difficult with the buses.
Carol: That's no problem. <u>I'll be driving</u> into town anyway. I'll take you.

Steve könnte weiterfragen: 'Are you driving back?' oder 'Will you be driving back?' Was ist der Unterschied?

Ask for help in a similar way in the following situations.

1. You want to use your friend's bike tomorrow afternoon.
   ..... your bike tomorrow afternoon? (you/use)
2. Your friend is going shopping. You want some stamps from the post office.
   .....? (pass/post office)

Now offer to help.

3. 'I have to give a message to Don, but he isn't on the phone.'
   'That's no problem. I ..... (see/this afternoon).
4. 'I need some eggs, but I can't leave the house.'
   'That's ...... I ..... (go shopping/soon).

§ 7 Das future perfect

Das ***future perfect*** wird benutzt für:

The concert **won't have finished** by nine.
The concert **will have started** by the time we arrive.
Will the concert **have finished** by ten?

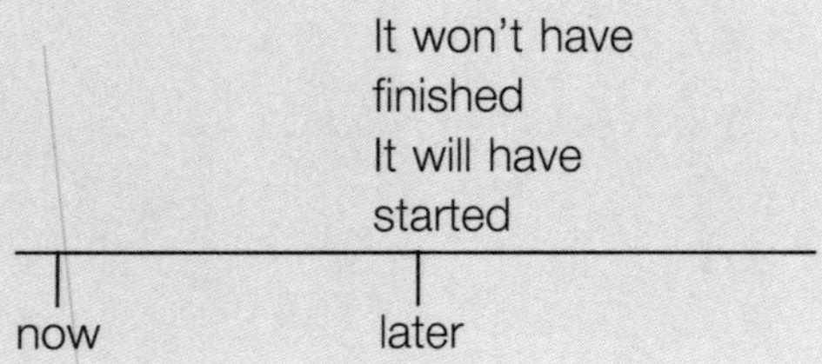

1. Aussagen oder Erkundigung darüber, ob ein Vorgang zu einem bestimmten Zeitpunkt in der Zukunft abgeschlossen sein wird oder nicht, immer mit der Zeitbestimmung.

By six o'clock Sue **will have been dancing** for 48 hours.

2. Vorgänge, die zu einem bestimmten Zeitpunkt in der Zukunft schon seit einiger Zeit andauern, von der Zukunft aus gesehen.

!

At six Sue will still be dancing.
(Von der Gegenwart aus gesehen: man weiß noch nicht, wie lange es dauern wird).
By six Sue will have been dancing for 48 hours.
(Von der Zukunft aus gesehen: man weiß, wie lange es schon gedauert hat).

Übung 11

Explain in German the differences between these sentences. Which rules help you to explain?

1. I'll fly to America next summer.
2. I am going to fly to America next summer.
3. I am flying to America next summer.
4. I fly to America next summer.
5. I'll be flying to America next summer.

Übung 12

The youth club have got a new room. What do you think they will have done to make it nicer two months from now?

Übung 13

Choose the correct future form to complete these sentences. Write down the number of the rule which helped you.

1. John can't come on Sunday. He ..... his girlfriend to decorate. (will help/is helping)
2. I'm sure you ..... your exam. (will pass/are passing)
3. Caroline ..... for the school team on Friday. (will play/is playing)
4. The weather ..... better tomorrow. (gets/will get/is getting)
5. When ..... the shops .....? (do ..... close/will ..... close)
6. 'I haven't got enough money for the bus,' 'It's ok. I ..... you some. (am going to lend/ will lend)
7. We won't catch the bus if we ..... hurry. (don't/won't)
8. How long ..... you .....? (do ..... stay/are ..... staying)
9. I ..... my homework by seven. (will finish/will have finished)
10. This time next year I won't be at school. I ...... (will work/will be working)
11. The last bus ..... at 11.30. (is leaving/leaves/will leave)
12. Shall we go for a coffee when the film ..... over? (is/will be)
13. In five years time I probably ..... with my parents any more. (won't live/won't be living)
14. Don't ring after eleven because I ..... to bed. (will go/will have gone)
15. If the bus ..... soon we'll have to get a taxi. (won't come/doesn't come)
16. What time ..... the train .....? (does ..... arrive/will ..... arrive)

6. Modals

Was sind **modale Hilfsverben,** und wozu braucht man sie?

Modale Hilfsverben sind sehr wichtig, um Einstellungen zu bekunden, z. B. um auszudrücken, daß etwas möglich, notwendig, empfehlenswert ist, oder um eine bestehende oder mangelnde Bereitschaft zu zeigen. Der Satz ***Mike . . . . . ring his girlfriend*** kann z. B. mehrere ganz verschiedene Bedeutungen haben, je nachdem, welches modale Hilfsverb eingesetzt wird:

	Mike **might** ring her.
	Mike **has to** ring her.
Mike . . . . . ring his girlfriend.	Mike **should** ring her.
	Mike **shouldn't** ring her.
	Mike **ought to** ring her.
	Mike **won't** ring her.

Der Unterschied ist doch sehr wichtig, oder nicht?
Fällt es Ihnen leicht, die verschiedenen Bedeutungen der modalen Hilfsverben richtig zu interpretieren und auch anzuwenden? Prüfen Sie erst einmal nach, was Sie schon können.

Überprüfen Sie Ihr Wissen

Test 1

Complete the following sentences, using 'be able to, can't have, could have, might be (-ing), might have, must, must be (-ing), must have, should be (-ing), shouldn't have'. Use each once only.

Example:
Mary's car is still outside. I don't think she can have gone to work.

1. Mary's car is still outside. She ..... to work. (go)
2. The curtains are drawn. Carol ..... still ..... in bed. (be)
3. The windows are shut. Brian ..... out. (go)
4. The Brands are taking suitcases to their car. They ..... on holiday. (go)
5. 'Do you know where Leslie is?' 'I'm not sure. She ..... to the youth club. Have you looked there?' (go)
6. 'Do you know where Leslie is?' 'I'm not sure. She ..... table-tennis.' (play)
7. I'm so tired this morning. I ..... so late last night. (stay up)
8. What is Kay doing here? She ..... her homework. (do)
9. My sister is learning Spanish. When we go on holiday next year she ..... it. (speak)
10. 'Did you go to Joe's party?' 'No, I ....., but I didn't want to.' (go)

Test 2

Translate the following sentences into English.

1. „Hättest du Lust, schwimmen zu gehen?"
   „Nein, ich mag jetzt nicht."
2. Soll ich dir eine Zeitung mitbringen?
3. „Ich muß jeden Tag um sieben aufstehen."
   „Ich brauche nicht so früh aufzustehen."
4. Leider konnte ich gestern nicht anrufen. Ich mußte weg.
5. Unsere Freunde sollten morgen ankommen.
6. Unsere Freunde hätten gestern ankommen sollen.
7. Ich werde versuchen, deinen Kassettenrekorder zu reparieren. Das dürfte nicht allzu schwierig sein.
8. Du brauchst nicht einkaufen zu gehen. Ich habe alles mitgebracht.
9. Mit diesem Schnupfen darfst Du nicht einkaufen gehen.
10. Mit diesem Schnupfen solltest Du nicht einkaufen gehen.

War das schwierig? Dieses Kapitel wird Ihnen helfen, in Zukunft keine Fehler mehr zu machen.

Grammatikregeln und Übungen

§ 1 Can – could – could have

A. can

Can you use a computer? (= Do you know how to?) I **can't** ride a bike.	1. Vorhandene oder nicht vorhandene Fähigkeiten
Can I use your computer? (= Will you allow me to?) – No, you **can't.**	2. Erlaubnis erbitten und erteilen oder vorenthalten Unklarheiten werden durch Umschreibung mit *know how to, allow, be able to* usw. vermieden.
England **can** be very warm in summer.	3. Allgemeine oder gegenwärtige Möglichkeiten
Can I get you a coffee? I **can** baby-sit for you tonight, if you like.	4. Vorschläge, Angebote

B. could

Jane **could** read when she was four. We **couldn't** understand what Frank wanted to say.	1. Fähigkeiten, die man in der Vergangenheit besessen hat oder nicht. (Siehe [!] *able to*: § 1, E.)
There **could** be another rise in the price of petrol soon.	2. Zukünftige Möglichkeit
Could I use your phone?	3. Höfliche Fragen und Bitten *Could* klingt höflicher und nicht so aufdringlich wie *can*.
We **could** go on holiday together.	4. Vorschläge

C. could have

Why didn't you ring? We **could have** met you at the station.	Etwas ist nicht geschehen, obwohl die Gelegenheit oder Fähigkeit vorhanden war.

can't – can't have – couldn't have; be able to

Jane **can't** be ill. I saw her at the swimming pool half an hour ago.
Tony **can't have** enjoyed the match. He looks very miserable.

D. can't/can't have

Logische Schlußfolgerung: etwas ist unmöglich
Can't – siehe § 2. A, 3; § 3.

At last we **were able to / managed to persuade / succeeded in persuading** Cathy to come on holiday with us, but we **couldn't** persuade Eric.
Could you persuade Eric to go with you last year?

I've never **been able to** do maths.
When I've finished this course **I'll be able to** speak Spanish, hopefully.

Are you **able to** drive your mother's car?

Can you drive your mother's car?
a) = Do you **know how to** .....?
b) = Are you **allowed to** .....?

As a child I **was able to** skate all day.

As a child I **could** skate all day.
a) = it was **possible** (my feet didn't hurt/ there was enough ice .....)
b) = I was **allowed** to

E. be able to

1. In Aussagesätzen, die ausdrücken, daß etwas in der Vergangenheit gelungen ist, wird *could* durch *be able, succeed in* oder *manage to* ersetzt.
   In Fragen und verneinten Sätzen dagegen kann *could* verwendet werden.
2. Die *present perfect*- und *future*-Formen von *can* werden mit *be able to* gebildet.

!

Da *can/could* mehrere Bedeutungen haben (vgl. § 1.A–D), wird *be able to* manchmal vorgezogen, um Mißverständnisse zu vermeiden.

Prüfen Sie nun bitte nach, wieviel Sie gelernt haben.

Übung 1

Make suggestions, using 'could'.

Example:
What shall we do tonight? (disco) We could go to the disco.

1. When shall we have our party? (next Saturday)
   We .....
2. What shall I give my mother for her birthday? (book)
   You .....
3. What shall we have for lunch? (some hamburgers)
   We .....

Übung 2

You want to be very polite. What would you say?

Example:
You have missed the school bus. Your sister has a bike. (use)
Could I use your bike, please?

1. It is raining and you have to go out. Your father has an umbrella.
   ....? (borrow)
2. You want your brother to help you with your homework. (help)
3. You want to know something from a neighbour. (ask something)

Übung 3

What would you say in the following situations? Use the correct form of 'can' or 'be able to'.

1. You have just started a French course. You are going to France next year. What do you ask your teacher?
   ..... I ..... next year? (speak)
2. You are having a party, but there will be many more girls than boys. You tell your friend:
   You ..... come if ...... (bring) .....
3. You want to buy a scooter, but you have to save enough money first.
   You think you will have the money next year.
   I think I ..... next year. (buy)

Which rules helped you to choose the right modal?

Übung 4

Make the meanings of these sentences clearer by explaining them, using 'be able to' or 'be allowed to'.

1. James couldn't play football because he was ill.
   He ..... play.
2. James couldn't play football because his father wouldn't let him.
   He ..... play.

What could this sentence mean?

3. Can you come on holiday with us?
   a) .....
   b) .....

Übung 5

Translate the following sentences, using the correct form of 'can, could' or 'be able to'.

1. Kannst Du Französisch?
2. Vor zehn Jahren konnte ich ganz gut Französisch.
3. Du könntest eine bessere Stelle finden, wenn Du eine Fremdsprache lernen würdest.
4. Dürfte ich bitte Dein Fahrrad ausleihen?
5. Leihst Du mir Dein Fahrrad?
6. Ich darf nicht ins Kino.
7. Ich kann nicht ins Kino, ich habe zu viele Hausaufgaben.
8. Maria kann bald skifahren, wenn sie ein bißchen übt.
9. Als Kind bin ich sehr schnell gelaufen.
10. Ich konnte noch nie Tischtennis spielen.
11. Darf ich Ihnen die Tasche abnehmen?
12. Das kann nicht die richtige Antwort sein.

Write down the number of the rule which helped you to find the correct answer.

§2 Must – mustn't

I really **must** stop smoking.

Ties **must** be worn.

The neighbours are very noisy. They **must be having** a party.

You **must** work hard.

Look, that **must** be Kevin's girlfriend.

A. must

1. Notwendigkeit
   Siehe §4.A,2.
2. Auffordern, zwingen, verpflichten.
   Must ist eine sehr starke Anweisung. Der/die Angesprochene fühlt sich verpflichtet oder gezwungen. *Must* wird vornehmlich im formellen und geschriebenen Sprachgebrauch verwendet.
   Siehe §4.A,2.
3. Logische Schlußfolgerung:
   Gegenwart

   !

   Das Gegenteil von *must* ist nicht die Verneinung *must not*, sondern wird durch ein anderes Hilfsverb wie *can, should, need, don't have to* usw. ausgedrückt:
   You don't have to/needn't work so hard.
   (= Du mußt nicht/brauchst nicht so hart zu arbeiten.)
   That can't be his girlfriend.
   (= Das kann nicht seine Freundin sein.
   Vgl. § 1.D)

   That mustn't be = das darf nicht sein.

You **mustn't** cross the road when the lights are at red.
I **mustn't** forget to post Sue's letter.
It's a secret. You **mustn't** tell anyone.

B. mustn't

Verbieten
Eine sehr starke Anweisung bzw. Verpflichtung.

!

Mustn't darf nicht mit „muß nicht" verwechselt werden:
you mustn't = du darfst nicht
du mußt nicht = *you don't have to/needn't*
Siehe § 4.A,2.

Übung 6

What do you think the headmaster is saying?
These words will help you:
It doesn't matter/I/wear.
Your son/wear/school uniform.

Übung 7

What must or mustn't you do when you see these signs? Wherever possible write two sentences.

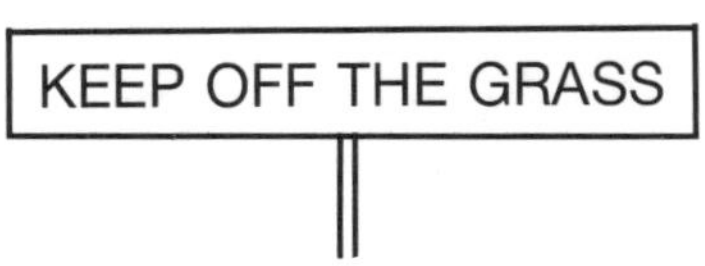

Tony .....
.... hamster

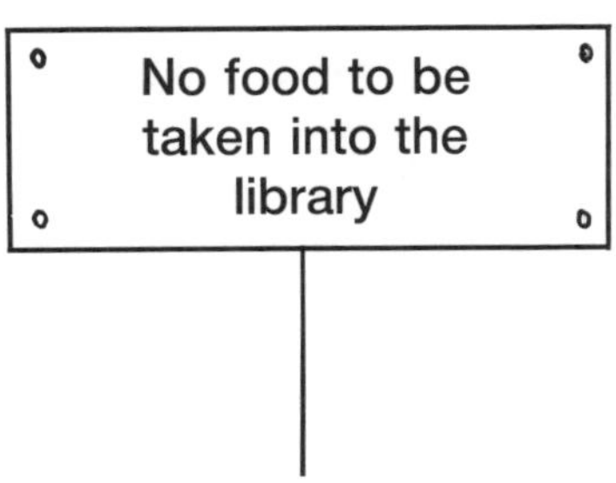

Übung 8

What is the difference between the following statements?

a) She isn't Spanish, she's Italian.
b) She can't be Spanish, she must be Italian.

Rewrite these sentences, using 'must' to suggest that something is very probable or 'can't' if something is not probable.

Example:
The baby keeps crying. I'm sure she's hungry.
The baby must be hungry.

1. Kay is out all the time. It is obvious that she knows a lot of people.
   Kay .....
2. Bill is always borrowing money. I'm sure he doesn't earn very much.
   Bill .....
3. What! You're tired already. But you've only just got up.
   You .....
4. There's the doorbell. I'm certain it's the postman.
   It .....

§3 Must have

David's late. He **must have** missed the bus.
Look, Leslie is still waiting for her friend. She **must have been** standing there all afternoon.

Logische Schlußfolgerung:
Vergangenheit.

!

In verneinten Sätzen verwendet man *can't have* (nicht *mustn't have*):
Kim passed me without speaking.
She can't have seen me.

Übung 9

Complete these sentences by using 'must be -ing, must have, can have' or 'can't have'.

1. Look at this book on Sheila's desk, 'French in Ten Days'. She ..... French. (learn)
2. I haven't seen Mrs Bond for ages. I think she ..... away. (go)
3. I wonder where Joe has put that magazine. Surely he ..... it away? (throw)
4. I don't believe you. You ..... (joke)
5. Ring the bell again. I don't think she ..... you. (hear)
6. The light was on in the kitchen this morning. I ..... to switch it off last night. (forget)

§4 Have to – not have to

Sorry, I **have to** go now.
Sorry, I**'ve got to** go now.
Do you really **have to** go?
Have you really **got to** go?
Why did you **have to** go to the doctor's?

A. have to

1. Auffordern; Notwendigkeit ausdrücken.

!

a) Zwischen *have to* und *have got to* gibt es keinen Bedeutungsunterschied. *Got* wird oft in der Umgangssprache vorgezogen, jedoch nur im *present tense*:
I've got to go to the doctor's.
I had to go to the doctor's yesterday.

'How do I get a passport?' –
'You **have to** fill a form in.'
(allgemeine Bestimmung)
'You**'ll have to** fill a form in.'
(in deinem, Ihrem speziellen Fall)

b) *have to/will have to*
Besonders in der gesprochenen Sprache wird *will have to* oft für spezifische Aufforderungen gebraucht, *have to* hat dagegen eine allgemeinere Bedeutung.

'Do you really **have to** go now?' 'Yes, I **have to** go and see my grandmother.' (= „**Mußt** Du ..... gehen?" „Ja, ich **muß** .....")

2. a) Vorsicht bei der Übersetzung von „müssen" im Präsens. *Must* wird nur für sehr starke Anweisungen und Verpflichtungen verwendet (vgl. §2). *Have to* ist die gängigere Übersetzung.

We **had to** wear ties to get into the disco.
My brother's ill. We**'ve had to** call a doctor.

b) Die *past tense* Formen von *must* werden mit *have to* gebildet.

B. not have to

I **didn't have to** wait long at the doctor's.
Mike **doesn't have to** go to work tomorrow.

Keine Notwendigkeit.
Vgl. *need not* §5.

Do I **have to** go?
You **don't have to** go.

!

Frage- und Verneinungssätze werden mit *to do* gebildet, im Gegensatz zu den anderen modalen Hilfsverben:
Can I go?

What time do you **have to** get up tomorrow?
I **must** get up early tomorrow.
(= I think it's necessary)
I **have to** get up early tomorrow.
(= Someone or something else makes it necessary)

Passengers **must** leave by the back-door.
Dogs **must** be kept on a lead.

C. have to – must

Auffordern; Notwendigkeit ausdrücken.
must wird dann gebraucht, wenn die Aufforderung zur Handlung vom Sprecher selbst ausgeht:
Dagegen drückt *have to* einen Zwang aus, der von anderen ausgeht.

Für Fremdsprachenlerner genügt es zu wissen, daß *have to* in der Umgangssprache bevorzugt wird, *must* dagegen kommt eher im offiziellen und im geschriebenen Sprachgebrauch vor.

Deutsche Sprecher neigen dazu, *must* viel zu häufig zu gebrauchen, das klingt aber für Briten sehr autoritär. Da *must* nur für sehr eindringliche Aufforderungen verwendet wird, ist es besser, in der Umgangssprache *have to* zu benutzen.

Übung 10

Complete these sentences by using 'must(n't)' or a form of 'have to'.

1. I'm sorry I couldn't come yesterday. I ..... take my motor bike to the garage.
2. My sister ..... to wear glasses since she was six.
3. You ..... forget to give your father the message. It's very important.
4. ..... you ..... change trains last night?
5. Why ..... Joan ..... go to the doctor's yesterday? – She cut her finger very badly.
6. ..... Tony ..... go to work by bus or can he walk it?
7. Why ..... Dennis ..... get up so early these days? – He ..... catch an earlier bus.
8. I can stay in bed tomorrow. I ..... go to school.
9. Children under 14 ..... be accompanied by an adult.
10. What ..... I ..... do to get a visa? ..... I ..... pay anything?
11. I can't stay any longer, I ..... be home by eleven.
12. All passengers ..... report to the information desk.

§5 Needn't/not have to – mustn't – needn't have – didn't need to

You **needn't/don't need to/don't have to** come with me if you don't want.
(= Du brauchst/mußt nicht)

A. needn't

Etwas ist nicht notwendig.
Zwischen *needn't, don't need to* und *don't have to* ist kein Bedeutungsunterschied.

You **mustn't** come with me.
(= Du darfst nicht)

B. mustn't

Must not darf nicht mit „muß nicht" verwechselt werden.

We **needn't have** booked seats.
(= But we did)

We **didn't need** to book seats.
(= So we didn't)

C. needn't have – didn't need to

Etwas wäre nicht notwendig gewesen:
needn't have

Etwas war nicht notwendig:
didn't need to

Übung 11

Explain the difference in each pair of sentences. Add something to each sentence to make the meaning clearer.

1. a) You mustn't shout at me.
   b) You needn't shout at me.
2. a) You mustn't tell Steve.
   b) You needn't tell Steve.

Übung 12

Rewrite these sentences so that they mean the same as the one above. Use 'not have to, needn't' or 'mustn't'.

Example:
I've already fed the cat. → You needn't feed the cat.

1. Don't eat all the biscuits.
   You ..... eat all the biscuits.
2. It is not necessary for you to get up early tomorrow.
   You ..... get up early tomorrow.
3. Wear a tie or not, just as you like. But no jeans.
   You ...., but you .... jeans.

Übung 13

In which of these sentences did the person actually walk/buy orange juice?

1. a) I needn't have walked all the way.
   b) I didn't need to walk all the way.
2. a) We didn't need to buy any orange juice.
   b) We needn't have bought any orange juice.

Übung 14

What did they say?

1. Valerie had no money, so she sold her stamp collection. A few days later she won a lot of money in a competition.
   'I . . . . . my stamps.'
2. Alan took his umbrella out with him, but it didn't rain.
   'I . . . . . my umbrella.'
3. Carol gave Mike a free ticket for a pop concert. The next day Mike told his mother:
   'It was free. I . . . . . pay.'

§6 May – might – may/might as well

I **may** decide to leave school next year.
You **may** be right.
We **may not** be able to get tickets for tonight.

A. may

1. Vermutungen; Möglichkeiten erwägen
   May darf nicht mit dem deutschen „mag" verwechselt werden:
   He may come = Vielleicht kommt er.
   (Nicht: er möchte kommen)

!

In Fragen wird *may* durch *can* oder eine andere Formulierung ersetzt:
That may be true.
Can that be true?
Is it possible that it's true?

May I have your attention, please?

2. Erlaubnis erbitten
   Heutzutage klingt es altmodisch und formell, wenn *may* gebraucht wird, um Erlaubnis zu erbitten oder zu erteilen. *May* in dieser Funktion wird durch *can/could* ersetzt. *(Can/Could I use your phone? – Yes, you can)*

B. might

You **might** say you're sorry.

I **might not** be able to come to the pop concert.

1. Ärger bekunden
2. Vermutungen, Möglichkeiten erwägen

C. may – might

'Do you think Alan will come to the party?'
a) He **may** do.
(neutrale Vermutung)
b) He **might** do.
(stärkere Unsicherheit)

My girlfriend **may** go to Scotland this summer.
(50% Wahrscheinlichkeit)

I **might** go with her.
(30% Wahrscheinlichkeit)

Der Bedeutungsunterschied zwischen *may* und *might* ist sehr gering.
May drückt eine größere Wahrscheinlichkeit aus.

D. may have – might have

I **may/might have** left my dictionary in the library.
'Julie's hair is wet.' – 'She **might have been swimming.'**

Vermutungen über vergangenes Geschehen
May drückt eine etwas größere Wahrscheinlichkeit aus, aber der Bedeutungsunterschied ist gering.

E. may/might as well

There's nothing to do. We **may/might as well** go home.
'Shall we go out?' 'Why not? We **may/might as well**.'

Der Sprecher steht dem Vorschlag gleichgültig gegenüber.

Übung 15

Express these ideas in a different way, using 'can' or 'may/might'

1. It is possible for me to leave school next year.
   I ....
2. It is possible that I will leave school next year.
   I ....
3. There is a chance that cigarettes will damage your health.
   Cigarettes ....
4. It has been found that cigarettes damage your health.
   Cigarettes ....

Übung 16

Sally hasn't arrived at school yet. What possible explanations can you think of? Use 'might (not), might (not) have' or 'might have been -ing'.

Example:
Perhaps she has missed the bus.
She might have missed the bus.

1. Perhaps she is not coming today.
   ....
2. Perhaps she is ill.
   ....
3. Perhaps she has gone to the doctor's.
   ....
4. Perhaps she didn't hear the alarm.
   ....
5. Perhaps she was dancing all night.
   ....

Übung 17

Rewrite these sentences, using 'might have, must have' or 'can't have'.

Sue knows our secret.

a) I'm sure Mike told her. Mike ....
b) Perhaps Mike told her. Mike ....
c) I know Mike hasn't talked to her yet. Mike ....

§7 Shall/should – should have – be to/be supposed to – ought to – had better

A. shall

Shall I get you a cup of tea?
Where **shall** we go?
Who **shall** we invite to the party?

Vorschläge, Angebote machen oder erbitten.

B. should

I think we **should** invite Ken to our party. He hasn't got many friends.
What do you think I **should** do?

1. Rat oder Vorschläge geben oder erbitten. Im Gegensatz zu *shall* impliziert *should* eine Verpflichtung, z. B. moralischer, rechtlicher Art.

You **should** enjoy the film. It's very funny.
The meeting **shouldn't** go on for too long.

2. Vermutungen: etwas ist wahrscheinlich.

'Go and get me a newspaper.' – 'Why **should** I?'
'Where's my purse?' – 'How **should** I know?'

3. Ärger bekunden.

You **should be doing** your homework, not listening to records.
You **shouldn't** speak to your parents like that.

4. Raten, warnen, tadeln.
Vgl. *ought to* (§7.E).

I **shouldn't** really be telling you this. (= But I am)

5. Die Absicht, Verpflichtungen oder Ratschläge zu ignorieren.

C. should have

I **should have** worked harder, then I might have passed the exam.

Verpflichtungen, denen man nicht nachgekommen ist.

D. be to/be supposed to

New pupils **are to** report to the headmistress at nine.
'Did you see the notice? We**'re supposed to** go and see Mrs Dean at nine.'

Are to und *be supposed to* drücken eine Verpflichtung aus, die z. B. durch eine Regel oder Vereinbarung festgelegt ist. *Are to* wird eher im offiziellen Sprachgebrauch verwendet, *be supposed to* ist informeller.

E. ought to – ought to have

We **ought to** be very careful not to destroy the world we live in.

Vgl. § 7. B,4.
Es ist kein großer Bedeutungsunterschied zwischen *should* und *ought to. Ought to* drückt eine stärkere Verpflichtung aus, z. B. moralischer oder rechtlicher Art.

I **should** really do my homework, but I **ought to** help my mother.

Die Verpflichtung, der Mutter zu helfen, wird als stärker empfunden.

Our new neighbours don't know many people yet. Perhaps we **ought to have** invited them to our party.

F. had better

You **had ('d) better** hurry up. (= Or something unpleasant will happen)
We**'d better not** go into that field. There's a bull in it.

Raten, warnen, tadeln. *Had better* drückt eine stärkere Verpflichtung oder Warnung aus als *should* oder *ought to.*

Übung 18

Some of these signs tell you that you must or must not do certain things, others only suggest you should or should not do them. Put in 'must, mustn't, should' or 'shouldn't'.

You ..... go jogging.

You ....

Cigarettes are dangerous

You ....

NO SMOKING

You ....

When there is a choice, for example if we can choose whether to go jogging or not, we use ..... (should/must).

Übung 19

Translate the following sentences, using 'shall, should, ought to' or 'should have'.

1. „Diese Mathematikhausaufgaben sind sehr schwierig." „Soll ich Dir helfen?"
2. Meine kleine Schwester hätte schon vor einer Stunde zu Hause sein sollen. Glaubst Du, wir sollten die Polizei anrufen?
3. „Ich kenne eine sehr arme Familie." „Du solltest ihr etwas Geld geben!"
4. Eigentlich sollte ich meine Hausaufgaben machen, aber ich habe keine Lust dazu.
5. „Welche Telefonnummer hat Ken?" „Wie soll ich das wissen?"
6. Dieser Film müßte dich interessieren. Er ist über Großbritannien.
7. Die Leute sollten langsamer fahren.
8. Paß auf, daß du die Tasse nicht zerbrichst.

Übung 20

What did the lions say? Use a form of 'should'.
"I suppose it would have been better if we hadn't done it".

I suppose ________________________________
really – they're terribly fattening

§8 Will

A. will

Will you come out with me on Saturday?

1. Bitten

'There's someone at the door,' – 'It **will be** the postman.'

2. Vermutung: etwas ist sicher aufgrund einer logischen Schlußfolgerung.

I'll help you.
Will you have a cup of tea?

3. Vorschläge, Angebote

Tony **won't** help me, but maybe Sue **will.**
My camera **won't** work.

4. Bestehende oder mangelnde Bereitschaft. Im übertragenen Sinne auch für Nichtbelebtes.

I **will** climb that mountain, just wait and see.

5. Entschlossenheit.
In diesem Zusammenhang wird 'will/won't' betont.

If you drop an egg it **will** break.
Some people just **won't** stop worrying.

6. Typische Verhaltensweisen oder Eigenschaften

!

Die Vergangenheitsform von *will* ist *would*:
Tony wouldn't help me last night.
I asked Carol if she would go out with me, but she refused.

Übung 21

Complete these sentences by using the correct form of 'will', 'won't' or 'would'.

1. 'We haven't got any bread.' 'I ..... go and get some.'
2. My cassette recorder ..... work. Can you repair it?
3. ..... you baby-sit for me tonight?
4. ..... you baby-sit for me tonight, please?
5. We told Dave he should work harder for the exam, but he ..... listen. Now he's failed.
6. I ..... win this match if it's the last thing I do. I ..... lose again. (not/want)
7. My friend is a vegetarian. She ..... eat any meat at all.
8. 'The phone's ringing.' 'It ..... be Jean. She's gone away this weekend.'

§9 Want – would

B. want

Will you come with me?
(= eine Bitte)
Do you **want to** come with me?
(= Hast Du Lust?)

will darf nicht mit *want to* verwechselt werden.

C. would

Would you help me with my homework, please?

1. Höfliche Bitten
   Vgl. §8. A, 1. *Would* klingt höflicher und weniger aufdringlicher als *will*.

Would you like a cup of tea?

2. Vorschläge, Angebote
   Vgl. §8.A, 3; §8.C, 1
   Would klingt höflicher und weniger aufdringlich als 'will'.

I'd like to go to England in the summer.

3. Wünsche

I'd rather go to Italy.

4. Vorlieben

A holiday in England **would** be nice.

5. Sich etwas vorstellen

Übung 22

What does Andy's wife say? Use 'would' and 'might'

[1]effort – the food I made for you
[2]tasty – good (tastes good)

7. Infinitive – ing-form

Haben Sie manchmal Schwierigkeiten mit Sätzen wie den folgenden? Wissen Sie oft nicht, ob man einen **Infinitiv** mit ***to*** oder ohne ***to*** gebraucht oder ob man eher die **ing-Form** verwendet?

There's a lot of **work to be done.**
Angela **wants me to marry** her.
My parents won't **let me stay** out overnight.
Linda waited **for** her boyfriend **to come.**
A map is used **for finding** directions.
I **remember buying** my first record.
I **remembered to buy** the record.
I watched Sue **mend** her bike.
I watched Sue **mending** her bike.

In diesem Kapitel finden Sie alles, was Sie wissen müssen, um den Infinitiv und die ing-Form richtig anwenden zu können.

Überprüfen Sie Ihr Wissen

Test 1

Complete these sentences by using the correct form of the verb in brackets.

1. 'Have you finished ..... this book'? (read) 'Yes, do you want ..... it?' (borrow)
2. 'The doctor has advised me ..... so hard. (not/work).' 'Why not ..... a holiday, then?' (take)
3. 'There's no point in ..... to the cinema now. (go) It's too late.' 'Well, what about ..... television, then?' (watch)
4. That film is not worth ..... (watch)
5. We've decided ..... to the pop concert, after all. (not/go)

6. Marion's parents won't let her ..... to the concert. (go)
7. After ..... for six months Christine has finally succeeded in ..... a job. (look, find)
8. I'm sorry about ..... the coffee on your shirt. (spill)
9. 'You don't look well. You'd better ..... at home today.' (stay) 'No, I'd rather ..... to school. I'll be alright.' (go)
10. Brenda seems ..... on holiday. She's very brown. (be)
11. Sally doesn't like dogs. She is afraid of ..... (bite)
12. 'Your hair needs .....' (cut) 'You know I can't stand ..... what to do.' (tell)
13. My friend is always trying to make me ..... new clothes. (buy)

Test 2

Translate the following sentences into English.

1. Hast du dich schon entschieden, was du tun willst?
2. Hast du jemanden, mit dem du reden kannst?
3. Wenn du willst, daß ich dir helfe, mußt du etwas warten.
4. „Wollen wir eine Tasse Tee trinken?" „Sehr gerne."
5. Wir warteten auf das, was kommen würde.

Test 3

Can you explain the difference between these pairs of sentences?

1. a) Do you like to dance?
   b) Would you like to dance?
2. a) Can you remember giving Mike five pounds?
   b) Can you remember to give Mike five pounds?
3. a) Julie stopped talking to her friend.
   b) Julie stopped to talk to her friend.
4. a) We watched the zoo keeper feed the animals.
   b) We watched the zoo keeper feeding the animals.

*War das sehr schwierig? Wiederholen Sie bitte zunächst die wichtigsten Regeln über den Gebrauch des Infinitiv mit **to**.*

Grammatikregeln und Übungen

§1 Der Infinitiv mit to

Der Infinitiv mit *to* steht in folgenden Konstruktionen:

1. Nach bestimmten Wörtern

a) Verben: *agree, appear, arrange, choose, decide, fail, help* (vgl. §2.3), *learn, manage, offer, plan, promise, refuse, seem, tend, want etc.*

Brenda has **arranged to see** the manager about an interview.
The job **seems to be** quite interesting.

b) Manchen Nomina

There's a lot of **work to be done.**

c) *Somebody, anything ...*

The new boy in our class has **no-one to talk to.**

d) Fragewörter/*whether*

Show me **what to do.**
Dave doesn't know **whether to leave** school or not.

e) Ordinalzahlen/*the only*

Sarah was the **first** girl **to win** a prize for science.

She was **the only** person from our school **to get** a prize

f) *too/enough*

It's **too** late **to get** tickets now.
Is it warm **enough to go out** without a coat?

2. Objekt + Verb + *to*

Nach Verben, die ein

a) Zulassen, Veranlassen oder einen Befehl ausdrücken:
advise, allow, ask, expect, invite, order, persuade, remind, teach, tell, warn etc.

My parents don't **allow me to smoke.**

Sue **persuaded Jill not to give up** her job.

Linda's mother **wants her to marry** Trevor.
Trevor **would like Linda to finish** her studies first.

b) Wünschen, Wollen, Mögen oder deren Gegenteil ausdrücken:
hate, hope, like, love, need, prefer, want, wish, would like/prefer etc.

!

Nach „wollen/mögen" steht im Deutschen ein Gliedsatz mit „daß". Dies verleitet zu dem Fehler, an *want* oder *would like* einen Gliedsatz mit *that* anzuschließen:
* Linda's mother wants that she marries .....

2.1 *like/want*
Like und *want* werden oft verwechselt.

Would you **like** to see my photos?
Do you **want** to see my photos?
(= Möchtest du meine Fotos sehen?)
Do you **like** to see my photos?
(= Siehst du sie gerne, normalerweise?)
When Martin was young he **wanted** to be a train driver.
Jean put her stamps away, but Steve **wanted** to look at them again.

Vermeiden Sie die Vergangenheitsformen von *like* immer dann, wenn statt dessen *wanted* eingesetzt werden kann.
Nicht
..... * he liked to be a train driver.
..... * Steve liked to look at them again.

2.2 *want/wish*
Want kann keinen irrealen Wunschsatz einleiten. Statt dessen steht *wish that*.

Mike **wanted to go** to the concert, but it was so bad he **wished that** he hadn't gone.

3. *for* + Objekt + *to*

Ann waited **for her boyfriend to come** out of the shop.
It's time **for me to go** to bed.
It's unusual **for the weather to be** so bad in August.

4. Der Infinitiv mit *to* drückt ein Ziel oder eine Absicht aus.

We stopped **to have** a drink.

!

Um Wiederholungen zu vermeiden, steht oft *to* anstelle von *to* + Verb.

'Do you want to come to town with me?'
'I'd love **to**.'

Übung 1

Translate the following sentences into English and write down the number of the rule which helped you. Always use infinitives.

1. Willst du mit mir tanzen? (höflich)
2. Ich habe Mike zum Tanzen aufgefordert, aber er wollte nicht. Ich wünschte, ich hätte ihn nie gefragt.
3. Meine Brieffreundin hat mich zu einem Ferienaufenthalt bei ihr eingeladen.
4. Werden deine Eltern die Kosten dafür übernehmen, daß du in den Ferien nach England gehst?
5. Die Lehrerin riet Thomas, nach Großbritannien zu gehen, um seine Englischkenntnisse aufzubessern.
6. Ist es für Ausländer leicht, in Großbritannien Ferienjobs zu bekommen?
7. Ich suche jemanden, der mir bei der Suche eines Ferienjobs hilft. Ich weiß nicht, wen ich fragen soll.
8. Es ist schwer für mich, mich auf englisch auszudrücken.
9. „Weißt du, wie man dieses Formular ausfüllt?“ „Nein, und es ist niemand da, den man fragen könnte.“
10. Kannst du warten, bis ich Geld gewechselt habe?
11. Susan wünschte, sie hätte John nicht zu ihrer Party eingeladen.
12. Willst du, daß ich früher komme?
13. „Will deine Schwester mitkommen?“ „Sie möchte gern, aber das will ich nicht.“

§2 Der Infinitiv ohne to

Der Infinitiv ohne ***to*** steht nach folgenden Verben bzw. Ausdrücken:

Kate **made Tony help** her with the housework.
Sue's parents **won't let her stay** out overnight.

1. Veranlassen, erlauben:
Make/let + Objekt + Infinitiv ohne *to*

'It's late. We**'d better go** home.'
'I**'d rather stay** a bit longer.'
Why pay more if you can buy it cheaper at this shop?

2. Nach *had better, would ('d) rather, why (not) . . .?*

Will you **help me to mend** my bike?
Will you **help me mend** my bike?

3. *help* + Infinitiv mit oder ohne *to*
Kein nennenswerter Bedeutungsunterschied.

Sind Sie sicher, wann man ***to*** vor den Infinitiv setzen muß und wann nicht? Prüfen Sie bitte nach.

Übung 2

Your British penfriend is staying with you. Compare the things you have to and don't have to do, at home and at school.

My parents Our teachers I/We	(don't)	make me/us ..... let me/us ..... allow me to/us to ..... have to .....

Write as many sentences as you can.

These words might help you: go to (parties .....)/go to bed, get up early, at ...../go out with ...../stay out ...../stay up late/in the week/at the week-end/bring friends home/do homework/two hours homework every day/speak English/be late/use biros/wear/smoke/ .....

Übung 3

Finish each of these sentences so that it means the same as the one before.

Example:

1. a) *Can I have your camera for a while?*
   Can you lend me your camera for a while? (lend)

   b) I don't like the idea of lending you my camera.
   I ..... you my camera. (not want/lend)

2. a) We are going to meet at the town hall
   We ..... at the town hall. (arrange/meet)

   b) Why don't you meet at the bus stop instead?
   Why not ..... at the bus stop instead? (meet)

3. a) We should get some more bread.
   We ..... some more bread. (had better/get)

   b) 'Will you get some more bread?' John asked Eric.
   John ..... some more bread. (ask/get)

4. a) What do you want to do, stay in or go out?
   ..... you ..... or .....? (would rather/stay in/go out)

   b) I'd rather stay in.
   I've ..... (decide/stay in)

§3 Die ing-Form (gerund)

Die **ing-Form** wird verwendet:

Do you **enjoy reading** comics?
I **don't mind not having** a television.
I **can't stand being told** what to do.

1. Nach bestimmten Verben:
avoid, dislike, enjoy, feel like, finish, go/keep (on), give up, imagine, mind, miss, practise, stop, suggest, can't help/stand etc.

Have you ever thought **of working** abroad?
Don't worry **about breaking** my record.
A map is used **for finding** directions.
Gerald had danced **without stopping** for four hours.

2. a) Präpositionen + -ing
agree with, ask/talk about, believe in, think of, pay for, look forward to, keep on, etc.
good at, happy/crazy/disappointed/excited/worried about, tired/proud/afraid of, interested in, keen on, used to/for etc.

After dancing all night Trevor was very tired.

b) Konjunktionen + -ing
after, although, before etc.

It's no use/no good talking to him. He doesn't listen.
Diane **couldn't help laughing.**
What about/How about going skating?
It's no fun walking about in the rain.
That film is**n't worth seeing.**

3. Nach bestimmten Wendungen:
it's no fun/good/use; it's (not) worth; can't help; what/how about .....?/ There's no point in .....

Your hair **needs cutting.**
This sweater **wants mending.**

4. *need/want* + -ing

Übung 4

Finish each of these sentences so that it means the same as the one before.

Example: *Which films do you like to watch? (enjoy)*
Which films do you enjoy watching?

1. It will be nice to lie on the beach. (look forward to)
I'm ..... on the beach.
2. It was strange for Thomas to drink tea with milk. (not used to)
Thomas was ..... tea with milk.

3. Would you like to listen to a record? (feel like)
   Do you ..... to a record?
4. Can you take me to town please? (would mind)
   ..... you ..... me to town, please?
5. Neil hates to be alone. (can't stand)
   Neil ..... alone.
6. Carol is happy when she is alone. (enjoy)
   Carol ..... alone.

Übung 5

How does the woman explain what happened to the sweater she made?

'The cat ... with the wool.'
(keep/play)

This cartoon is an example of rule § .....

Übung 6

Complete the following sentences by using the -ing form, infinitive with 'to' or without 'to'.

1. I don't know your boyfriend, but I'd like ..... him. (meet)
2. I'm looking forward to ..... your boyfriend. (meet) Why not ..... him round tonight? (bring)
3. My bike needs ..... (mend), but I don't know when ..... it. (do)
4. 'I'm tired of ..... so hard. (work) I want ..... (do) something different now.' 'What about ..... a film, then?' (see)
5. The film was so sad it made me ..... (cry)
6. Stop ....., will you? (cry)
7. 'What was the film about?' 'It's too difficult ..... (explain)
8. Can you write a letter in English without ..... a mistake? (make)
9. Barbara hasn't learned how ..... her computer yet. (use)

10. Bob can't stand ..... (be criticised)
11. 'There's no point in ....., let's go home.' (wait) 'I don't live far from here. It's not worth ..... on a bus.' (get)
12. You should give up ..... (smoke) The doctor has warned you ..... (not/smoke)
13. It's no good ..... about your exams. (worry) They're over now, so you'd better ..... them. (forget)
14. 'I'm fed up with ..... to school. (go) I'd rather ..... a job.' (get) 'Why not ..... school, then?' (leave)
15. 'What do you want to do after ..... school?' (leave) 'I'd like ..... abroad for a while.' (work)

Welche Sätze sind Beispiele für
(a) Regel §3.1? ....
(b) Regel §3.2? ....
(c) Regel §3.3? ....
(d) Regel §3.4? ....

Übung 7

Warum wird hier die ing-Form verwendet? Welche Regel gibt die Erklärung? §...

... as I was saying,
he's marvellous at carrying the shopping home,
unless we meet a cat...

§ 4 Verben mit Infinitiv und ing-Form

Auf manche Verben kann sowohl der **Infinitiv** als auch die **ing-Form** folgen:

We were just going out when it **started to rain/raining.**
They **don't allow smoking** in this part of the cafe.
They **don't allow you to smoke** in this part of the cafe.

1. Bei manchen Verben verändert sich die Bedeutung kaum, ganz gleich, ob dem Verb ein Infinitiv oder eine ing-Form folgt: *allow* (vgl. § 1.2a) *begin/start, continue, intend, like, love, hate, prefer*

I **like getting up** early.
(= ich mache es gern)
I **like to get up** early.
(= ich finde, das sollte ich tun)

!

Wenn *like* „gern machen" bedeutet, gebraucht man eher die ing-Form.
Wenn *like* bedeutet, daß man etwas für richtig hält, gebraucht man eher den Infinitiv.

2. Bei anderen Verben verändert sich die Bedeutung, je nachdem, ob darauf ein Infinitiv oder eine ing-Form folgt:

a) I still **remember/I'll never forget buying** my first record.

I **remembered/didn't forget to buy** the record.

a) *remember/forget* + ing-Form:
sich an etwas in der Vergangenheit erinnern
remember/not forget + Infinitiv:
sich erinnern, etwas zu tun

b) Tony **stopped eating** his ice-cream.

Tony **stopped to eat** his ice-cream.

b) *stop* + ing-Form:
aufhören, etwas zu tun
stop + Infinitiv:
aufhören, um etwas zu tun

c) 'I'm **trying to learn** Italian.'

'Have you **tried using** a cassette-recorder?'

c) *try* + Infinitiv:
versuchen, ein Ziel zu erreichen
try + ing-form:
eine bestimmte Methode ausprobieren

I **watched** Sue **mend** her bike. It didn't take long.
I **watched** Sue **mending** her bike for a few minutes, then I left.

3. Verben der Sinneswahrnehmung:
see, watch, hear, listen to, feel, smell
Mit Infinitiv: ein Vorgang wird insgesamt, einschließlich seines Ergebnisses, erfaßt.
Mit ing-Form: nur der Teil eines Vorgangs wird wahrgenommen, der sich gerade im Ablauf befindet, also noch nicht zu Ende ist.

Übung 8

Derek's parents are away on holiday. They gave him a list of things to do while they were away. What has he remembered to do? What has he forgotten?

1. He has . . . . (remember)
2. He has . . . . (forget)

   But his parents are not coming back until tomorrow, so he still has a little time. What does he say to himself?
3. I . . . . (must(n't) remember/forget)

Übung 9

You are sitting with an old friend remembering some of the things you once did together. Talk about your memories.

Example: *Do you remember being bitten by that dog? (bite/that dog)*
I'll never forget falling into the river (fall/river)

1. Do you remember . . . . ?
   (go into hospital/you were ten; want to be a doctor)
2. I'll never forget . . . .
   (learn to ride a bike; go out with a girl/boy for the first time)
3. I'll always remember . . . .
   (cry on my first day at school; earn my first money)

Write down some of the things that you remember or will never forget.

Übung 10

Which of the forms in brackets completes the sentences?

1. 'I've tried ..... this maths homework, but I can't.' (to do/doing)
   'Have you tried ..... Jill? She's very good at maths.' (to ask/asking)
2. 'I can't go to sleep at nights.' 'Have you tried ..... a drink of warm milk before you go to bed?' (to have/having)
3. Sue is trying ..... enough money to buy a motor bike. (to save up/saving up)
4. 'My radio isn't working.' 'Why don't you try ..... a new battery in?' (to put/putting)
5. Barbara stopped ..... and stood up. (to talk/talking)
6. Barbara stopped ..... to her friend who had just got off the bus. (to talk/talking)
7. Shall we stop ..... something to eat? (to have/having)
8. If you don't stop ..... soon I'll go mad. (to sing/singing)

Übung 11

Think carefully about whether you need the infinitive or the -ing form in these sentences.

1. I heard Trevor ..... his guitar yesterday. (play) He played for me all afternoon.
2. I heard Trevor ..... his guitar yesterday. (play) Unfortunately I couldn't stay long.
3. Did you hear someone ..... as we passed that window? (sing)
4. I saw Manchester United ..... against Liverpool last week. (play) It was a great match from beginning to end.
5. The missing boys were last seen ..... near the old farm. (play) A woman saw them on her way home from work.
6. 'How do you know I came in late?' 'I heard you ..... up the stairs and go to the bathroom.' (come)
7. Diane watched the car ..... round the corner and drive away. (turn)
8. I saw Elizabeth ..... in the park as I went past on my bike. (sit)
9. I saw Elizabeth ..... down on a bench and start talking to a young boy. (sit)

Which rule helped you? § .....

Übung 12

Can you work out what the first prisoner says?

'.........................'

(we're in time/being fed/them/
I hope/to see)

8. Participles

Es gibt zwei Arten von Partizipien:

1. das ***present participle:*** *making, sitting*
2. das ***past participle:*** *finished, pleased*

Das ***present participle*** hat eine aktive Bedeutung:
The girl telling the story is a famous actress.
(= The girl is doing something)

Das ***past participle*** hat eine passive Bedeutung:
Did you hear the story told by that famous actress?
(= Something is done to the story)

Vergleichen Sie bitte die folgenden Sätze und überlegen Sie dabei, worin der Vorteil der Partizipialkonstruktionen auf der rechten Seite besteht.

I know the girl who is playing table-tennis.	I know the **girl playing** table-tennis.
Jeff put down his book and looked at me in surprise.	**Putting down his book,** Jeff looked at me in surprise.
Frank fell asleep while he was watching the film.	Frank fell asleep **watching** the film.
Though she did not know what to expect, the detective pushed open the door.	**Though not knowing** what to expect, the detective pushed open the door.
Meat will go bad if it is not cooked immediately.	Meat will go bad **if not cooked** immediately.
Who's that boy who is standing near the door?	Who's that boy **standing** near the door?
There's a big car which is parked outside our house.	There's a big car **parked** outside our house.

Die Partizipialkonstruktionen sind kürzer und wirken geschliffener als die Sätze auf der linken Seite. Sie werden meistens im formellen, schriftlichen Sprachgebrauch eingesetzt. Es folgen einige weitere Beispiele für typische Partizipialsätze.

Not knowing what to do, we went to the police station.
Tony opened the door, **surprised** to see Jennifer.
No wonder you've got a headache **with** your brother **making** so much noise.
Although **done** by a child, the painting was extremely good.
Children not **allowed** unless **accompanied** by an adult.
Carol sat **reading** all afternoon.
Why don't you **get** your hair **cut?**
Talking of hair, have you **had** yours **dyed?**

Überprüfen Sie ihr Wissen

Test

Translate these sentences into German.

1. Hearing the doorbell, Ann ran downstairs.
2. Jill cut her finger mending her bike.
3. Can you introduce me to the girl sitting near the window, please?
4. Four boys were sitting on the floor playing cards.
5. After being shown round Maria's new flat we all agreed that it was beautiful.
6. Are you going to have the flat wallpapered or do it yourself?
7. Kevin stood looking at the painting, absolutely fascinated.
8. Don't you think Diane looks better with her hair hanging down her back?
9. I've left my umbrella standing in the hall.
10. Having spent a sleepless night, we were all very tired.
11. Though paid very little, Eric is enjoying his new job.
12. Being unemployed, Jenny doesn't have much money.
13. With prices rising every day, I'm surprised people can still afford to buy cars.
14. Worried about the interview the next day, Cathy could not sleep.
15. Drivers must not stop on the motorway unless forced.
16. How would you like to spend a weekend at a luxury hotel, with all expenses paid?

Grammatikregeln und Übungen

§1 Partizipien anstelle adverbialer Gliedsätze
§1.1 Nebensätze der Zeit

Partizipien können Nebensätze der Zeit ersetzen. Sie werden oft durch *when, while, after, having* eingeleitet.

Walking past Carol's house I saw her new bike in the garden.
(= when I walked past ...)

1. Wenn zwei Handlungen gleichzeitig stattfinden, kann der Temporalsatz durch eine Partizipialkonstruktion ersetzt werden.

Frank fell asleep (while) **watching** the film.

I hurt my foot (while) **jogging.**

2. Läuft eine Handlung gerade ab, wenn eine andere eintritt, kann die Handlung, die länger andauert, durch eine -ing Form ersetzt werden.

   Dabei kann *while* wegfallen, wenn dadurch keine Mißverständnisse entstehen (vgl. §1.1,4).

(After) having passed the final exams, Sue started to look for a job.
After watching the horror film Steve could not sleep.
Putting down his book, Jeff looked at me in surprise.

3. Wenn eine Handlung vor einer anderen stattfindet, kann die erste durch eine Partizipialkonstruktion ausgedrückt werden.

Susan waved to John **riding** past on a bike.
a) **Susan** waved to John while **riding** past.
(= Susan was riding)
b) Susan waved to **John, who was riding** past.
(= John was riding)

4. Mißverständnisse
   Manchmal muß die Partizipialkonstruktion durch *when* oder *while* eingeleitet werden, um klarzustellen, worauf sich der Partizipialsatz bezieht.

§ 1.2 Andere Nebensätze: Grund, Begleitumstände, nach ‚with', Einschränkung, Bedingung, Relativsätze

Ein Partizipialsatz kann auch andere Nebensätze ersetzen.

Not knowing what to do, we went to the police station.
Having already seen the film, I did not want to go again.

1. Grund
Partizipialkonstruktionen werden gebraucht, um Erklärungen abzugeben. Sie stehen meistens am Satzanfang und werden oft durch ein Komma abgetrennt.

Tony opened the door, **surprised** and **pleased** to see Jennifer.

2. Begleitumstände werden oft durch Partizipien ausgedrückt (vgl. „indem, wobei"). Die *-ing form* folgt oft nach Verben der Bewegung:
come, go, hurry, run, walk etc.

a) No wonder you've got a headache **with** your brother **making** so much noise.
(= wenn Dein Bruder . . .)
b) The best pupils in the school can go to America for a month **with** all expenses **paid.**
(= wobei)

3. Partizipialsätze nach *with* sind in der Umgangssprache sehr häufig. Sie drücken oft Gründe (a) oder Begleitumstände (b) aus. Solche Konstruktionen werden oft mit „wenn, wobei (jedoch), da, und, während, jetzt/heutzutage wo, damals als" übersetzt.

Although done by a child, the painting was extremely good.
Though not knowing what to expect, the detective pushed open the door.

4. Einschränkungen können durch Partizipialsätze ausgedrückt werden. Sie werden durch *(al)though* eingeleitet.

Meat will go bad **if not cooked** immediately.
Children not allowed **unless accompanied** by an adult.
(= if they are not with)

5. Bedingungen werden oft durch Partizipien ausgedrückt. Sie können mit *if* oder *unless* eingeleitet werden.

Who's that boy **standing** near the door?
There's a big car **parked** outside our house.

6. Relativsätze werden oft durch Partizipialsätze ersetzt.

Nun prüfen Sie nach, wieviel Sie gelernt haben.

Übung 1

Make one sentence out of two, using an -ing form.

Example:
Ken was sitting in the kitchen. He was talking to Jean.
Ken was sitting in the kitchen talking to Jean.

1. Alan was lying on his bed. He was listening to the radio.
2. Jeff broke his leg. He was skiing.
3. Sue heard the phone ring. She got up to answer it.
4. I got home. I was feeling tired.
5. I walked past the shop. I remembered I needed some milk.

In Satz 3 findet eine Handlung vor einer anderen statt. Woher wissen Sie, welche Handlung durch eine -ing Form ausgedrückt werden kann? Welche Regeln helfen Ihnen? Welche Regeln helfen Ihnen bei den anderen Sätzen?

Übung 2

"It IS me. I got the beard waiting out there for my flight."

Which words could you add to what this man is saying?

Übung 3

Put brackets round the parts of the sentences which could be left out.

Example:
Have you seen a girl (who is) wearing a green coat?

1. My cousin lives in a house which was built a hundred years ago.
2. Everyone who is going on the coach trip should be here by seven.
3. The accident was seen by several people who were waiting at the bus stop.
4. Letters which are posted before six o'clock will be delivered the following day.

Übung 4

Can you describe these drawings? These words will help you: bear, bike, climb, giraffe, Mexican, ride, tree, walk, window.

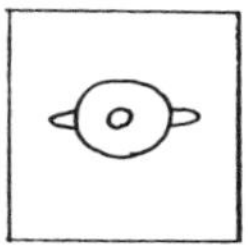

a . . . . .ing a . . . . .

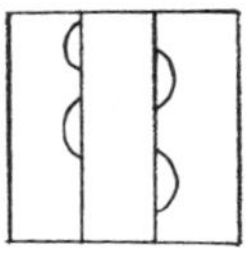

a . . . . .ing a . . . . .

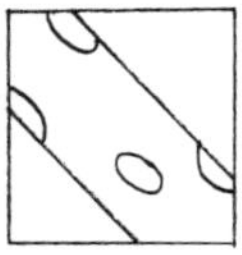

a . . . . .ing . . . . . a . . . . .

Exercises 3 and 4 are examples of rule § . . .

Übung 5

Rewrite the underlined parts of these sentences using 'with' and a participle.

Example:
You can't go to school if your head is aching like that.
with your head aching like that.

1. I can't read the paper if you interrupt me all the time.
2. Because travel is becoming cheaper more and more people are going abroad for their holidays.
3. Since there are only a few more minutes left our team must try to score a goal.
4. There's a good bus service to town: buses run every ten minutes.

Übung 6

Translate the following sentences.

1. Having worked in America for two years, my sister has a lot of friends there.
2. Hearing a noise, Tony woke up.
3. Sue ran out of the house, banging the door after her.
4. I couldn't leave my brother alone yesterday with him feeling ill.
5. Can you smell something burning?
6. Cleaned and painted, that bike would look as good as new.
7. The dog came running up to us.
8. Being a foreigner, you need a visa to stay in this country.
9. Asked what she thought of the exam, Maria said it was too easy.
10. Though surprised, Carol said nothing.
11. Alan put the phone down, disappointed that Dave couldn't come.
12. This can will explode if left in a warm place.
13. The lake looks lovely with the sun shining on it.

§2 Partizipien nach bestimmten Verben

Carol **sat reading** all afternoon.
I've been **standing waiting** for you for ages.

1. Nach Zustandsverben wie *lie, sit, stand, stay* steht oft die *ing-form.*

Don't let me **catch** you **reading** my letters again.
I'm sorry I **kept** you **waiting.**
Why do you always **leave** your things **lying** about?
Does your mother always **send** you **shopping?**

2. Nach *catch, keep, leave, send.*

Why don't you **have/get** your hair **cut?**

Eric has **had** his money **stolen.**
(*get* würde heißen, er hat es absichtlich stehlen lassen!)

I really must **get** my watch **repaired.**

I really must **get** my homework **done.**

3. Nach *have/get* mit der Bedeutung „etwas machen/besorgen lassen".
Der Bedeutungsunterschied zwischen *have* und *get something done* ist gering.
Have bedeutet aber oft, daß etwas Unangenehmes passiert
get deutet daraufhin, daß die Handlung etwas Mühe kostet.

!

To get something done kann auch bedeuten, daß man die Handlung selbst ausführt.

Übung 7

Ken is always complaining. Look at the things he keeps saying to his girlfriend.

Ken:
- You always keep me ..... (wait).
- You always leave the radio ....., even when you're not listening to it (switch on).
- You keep ..... my library books (read).
- I don't want to catch you ..... my comb again (use).
- You sit ..... nothing all the time (do) and I've been standing ..... records in the shop all day (sell).
- Why don't you get your hair ..... (cut)? It looks awful!

Ann:
- Why don't you get yourself another girlfriend, Ken? Goodbye.

§3 Idiomatische Wendungen mit Partizipien

Considering that Gordon has only been doing English for two years he's very good.
Talking of Jenny, I haven't seen her lately.

Partizipien in einigen Redewendungen: *considering, generally speaking, strictly speaking, judging from, seeing that, supposing, talking of, weather permitting, provided/ providing that . . .*
Solche partizipialen Wendungen werden durch Kommas abgetrennt.

Übung 8

Use each expression once to complete the sentences:
generally speaking, judging from, seeing that, supposing, weather permitting.

1. We'll have a picnic on Saturday, ...
2. . . . . . you won't be using your bike this afternoon, can I borrow it?
3. I don't, ..., like westerns.
4. . . . . . they were to offer you the job, would you take it?
5. Linda's just had a shock, ... the look on her face.

9. If-clauses

Wozu brauchen wir ***if***-Sätze?
Schauen Sie sich bitte die folgenden Beispiele an.

If you give me your stamps you can have my posters.
If you break my record you'll have to buy me another.
I'll help you if you wait a minute.
If our house were on fire I would call 999.

Die Information, die uns am wichtigsten ist, steht am Satzanfang:

Vgl. **You can have my poster** if you give me your stamps.

Man braucht ***if***-Sätze immer dann, wenn
Sachverhalte oder Ereignisse <u>von bestimmten Bedingungen abhängig</u> sind.

Solche Bedingungen können in drei Haupttypen eingeteilt werden:

I : If I **do** A, then B **will/can/might/must/should happen.**
If A **happens**, then **do** B.

II : If I **did** A, then B **would/could/might ..... happen.**

III: If I **had done** A, then B **would/could/might ..... have happened.**

Überprüfen Sie Ihr Wissen

Test 1

Translate the following sentences into English.

1. Falls ich Zeit habe, helfe ich dir.
2. Wenn ich Zeit habe, helfe ich dir.
3. Wenn ich den Bus verpasse, nehme ich ein Taxi.
4. Ich gehe nicht zu deinen Freunden, es sei denn, man lädt mich ein.
5. Ich gehe auch dann nicht, wenn ich eingeladen werde.
6. Mein Vater redet mit mir, als ob ich ein Kind wäre.

Test 2

In welchen der folgenden Sätze glaubt man eher, daß die Ereignisse im if-Satz (die Bedingungen) eintreten könnten?
In welchen Sätzen ist man sich nicht so sicher?

1. If Brenda invites me to her party I'll go.
2. If Brenda invited me to her party I would go.
3. If the train arrives on time I'll be very surprised.
4. If the train arrived on time I would be very surprised.

Test 3

Complete these sentences by using the correct forms of the words in brackets.

1. Will you write to me if I ..... you my address? (give)
2. Would you write to me if I ..... you my address? (give)
3. If Jill ..... her bike she won't get much for it. (sell)
4. If Jill ..... her bike she wouldn't get much for it. (sell)
5. If Jill ..... her bike she wouldn't have got much for it. (sell)
6. If they offered Sally the job ..... she ..... it? (take)
7. If they had offered Sally the job ..... she ..... it? (take)
8. Mike talks to Diane as if she ..... a child. (be)
9. If I only ..... Tina's address. (have)
10. I'll phone her when she ..... home. (get)
11. If the car ..... we would have gone on holiday last week. (not/break down)
12. If you ..... wear such long skirts you would look much better. (not/wear)
13. If we ..... to see old Mr Spinks he would be very pleased. (go)
    Shall we go tomorrow?
14. If Jane ..... to bed earlier last night she wouldn't be so tired today. (go)
15. If Kevin had worked harder he ..... the test. (might/pass)
16. What would you be doing now if we ..... to see you? (not/come)
17. If I ..... English better I would be very happy. (can/speak)

Grammatikregeln und Übungen

§ 1 If, when

Im Englischen gibt es zwei Wörter für das deutsche „wenn“:
if, when(ever).

If I have time I'll help you.
When I have time I'll help you.
Whenever I have time I'll help you.

I'll help you_if I have time.

Kann man „wenn“ durch „falls“ ersetzen , so benutzt man *if*.
„Falls ich Zeit habe .....“
„Wenn ich Zeit habe .....“
„Wann immer ich Zeit habe .....“
Durch Umstellung des *if*-Satzes betont man eher den Hauptsatz:
I'll help you if/when/whenever I have time.

!

Im Gegensatz zum Deutschen steht im Englischen kein Komma vor dem if-Satz.

Übung 1

Translate these sentences into English, using 'if', 'when' or 'whenever'.

1. Wenn ich in die Stadt gehe, bringe ich dir eine Zeitschrift mit.
   a) (Marion ist sicher, daß sie hingeht)
      Marion: '..... I go to town .....'
   b) (Marion weiß nicht, ob sie hingeht)
      Marion: '..... I go to town .....'
2. Immer, wenn ich in die Stadt gehe, bringe ich meiner Mutter eine Zeitschrift mit.
3. Wenn ich älter bin, will ich Popstar werden.
4. Wir sind nicht sicher, ob wir nach Irland fahren. Aber wenn wir hinfahren, dann für drei Wochen.
5. Immer, wenn wir nach Irland fahren, besuchen wir meinen Brieffreund.
6. „Habe ich meinen Schlüssel bei dir liegenlassen, als ich heute morgen vorbeikam?“
   „Ich glaube nicht, aber wenn ich ihn finde, rufe ich dich an.“
7. Immer, wenn ich Bilder von New York sehe, möchte ich hinfahren.
8. Was würdest du tun, wenn du von einem Hund gebissen würdest?
9. „Was machen wir, wenn wir den Zug verpassen?“

Es ist nicht immer ganz einfach, nach ***if*** die richtige Zeitform des Verbs zu finden. Zunächst einige Regeln.

§2 If-Sätze vom Typ I: wahrscheinliche Bedingungen

Typ I: If I **do** A, then B **will/can/might/must/should happen.**
If A **happens,** then **do** B.

a) **If** you **don't hurry** you'll miss the bus.
I can get a taxi **if** I **miss** the bus.
If Ann **is** still in hospital we could go and see her.

b) **If** Brian **is** still **having** a bath we'll have to go without him.
If Sally **is feeling** sick she should go and lie down.

c) **If** Tony **hasn't booked** his holiday yet he ought to hurry.
If the train **has arrived** on time Aunt Mary will be here soon.

d) **If** you **miss** the bus **get** a taxi.
I Sally **is feeling** sick **tell** her to go and lie down.

1. Es werden Voraussetzungen oder Bedingungen genannt, unter denen etwas geschehen wird, kann, soll usw. Die Bedingungen werden für erfüllbar gehalten oder sind bereits erfüllt worden (reale Bedingungen):
es ist noch möglich, sich zu beeilen, den Bus zu verpassen, daß sie im Krankenhaus ist usw.

Je nachdem, ob sich die Bedingung auf ein künftiges Geschehen, ein Geschehen, das noch im Verlauf ist oder auf die Vergangenheit bezieht, steht im *if*-Satz das *simple present* (a), *present progressive* (b) oder das *present perfect* (c).

Im Satztyp *If A happens, then do B* steht im Hauptsatz ein Imperativ (d).

I won't go to the party **unless** I'm invited.
(= if I'm not invited)
I won't go **even if** I'm invited.

2. *Unless, even if*
Bedingungssätze können auch durch *unless* („wenn nicht") und *even if* („auch dann, wenn .....") eingeleitet werden.

§3 Will, should in Bedingungssätzen

will

will wird in Bedingungssätzen oft falsch verwendet, z. B.:
*If I will miss the bus I can get a taxi.

will steht nach *if* nur mit folgender Bedeutung:

- Jemand will unbedingt etwas tun oder nicht tun; jemand pflegt, etwas zu tun, häufig in Verbindung mit Verben wie *insist, refuse*.

If Joe **will talk/will insist on talking** all the time he'll soon have no friends.
If Sally **will spend** so much money on clothes she'll soon have none left.

- Jemand ist willens oder bereit, etwas zu tun.
  Diese Regeln treffen sowohl für reale als auch irreale Bedingungen zu.
  (Vgl. §4,4–5)

If you **will** wait here a moment I'll get the manager.
If my father **will** lend me the car we'll go for a drive tonight.

should

Es wird für wenig wahrscheinlich gehalten, daß die Bedingungen erfüllt werden.

If there **should be** any problems let me know.
(= but I don't expect any)

!

If there are any problems .....
(= there might be some)

If I **shouldn't get** there on time don't wait for me.
(= but I don't expect to be late)

!

If I don't get there on time .....
(= I might not)

If kann auch weggelassen werden. Dann muß aber *should* vor dem Subjekt stehen.

Should there be any problems .....
Should I not get there on time .....

Übung 2

Put these two lists together and join them with the correct verb. At times you have to change the form of the verbs.

	~~too many sweets~~	ask her to give me a ring.
	to read this book	we should win.
	Sally tonight	can watch the match on TV.
	smoking	look to the right first.
If you	in our team	~~you'll get fat~~
	home early we	come and see me.
	this form	I'll lend it to you.
	some free time	you'll be ill.
	a road in Britain	you can join the library.

Verbs: come, cross, eat, fill in, have, play, not give up, see, want

Example: If you eat too many sweets you'll get fat.

Übung 3

Put the words in brackets into the correct tense.

1. Mike will soon have an accident if he ..... so fast. (drive)
2. Eric will never be ready on time if he ..... still ..... on the phone. (talk)
3. If the bus ..... soon I'll start walking. (not/come)
4. Julie won't give me my book back if I ..... her. (not/ask)
5. If you ..... a ticket for the play yet I don't think you'll get one any more. (not/buy)
6. If we ..... the play we'll leave before the end. (not/like)
7. If Jenny ..... to her records she won't hear us ringing the doorbell. (listen)
8. What! Linda is still in bed! I can't wait for her if she ..... yet. (not/get up). But if she ..... ready in ten minutes I'll give her a lift. (should/be)

Übung 4

Complete these sentences with 'if', 'even if' or 'unless'.

1. I'll forgive you ..... you say you're sorry.
2. You won't get a job ..... you have good qualifications. They are absolutely necessary.
3. ..... you have good qualifications it doesn't mean you will get a job.
4. Ring me ..... you need help.
5. Don't ring me ..... you need help. I'm very busy at the moment.
6. Ring me, ... it's late at night. I don't mind.

Übung 5

Brian went to see his friend, Angela. But she was not in. Write out the message he left her.

> If you ___ to come to the match
> with me tomorrow let me know. Ring me
> ___ you get home. If I ___ not in
> I'll be at my mother's.

§4 If-Sätze vom Typ II: irreale Bedingungen

Typ II: If I **did** A, then B **would/could/might . . . happen.**

If Steve **passed** the exam he **could get** the job.
(= but he probably won't)

1. Es ist zweifelhaft, ob die Bedingungen erfüllt werden (irreale Bedingungen).

If I **had** the money I would buy a bike.
(= but I don't have it)
If I **were** you I would change my hair-style.
(= but I am not you)

2. In bezug auf die Gegenwart ist es unmöglich, daß die Bedingungen erfüllt werden (irreale Bedingungen).

If our house **were/was** on fire I would call 999.

Bei *to be* wird in der Regel *I/he/she/it were* gebraucht, obwohl sich im gesprochenen Englischen *was* immer mehr durchsetzt.

If only I **knew** her phone number.
He talks to me **as if** I **were** a child.
She behaves **as if** she **owned** the place.

If-Sätze vom Typ II (und III) können auch durch *if only* und *as if* eingeleitet werden.

If only he **wouldn't** talk to me as if I were a child.
If only Ann **would** help me.

Nach *if only* kann auch *would* folgen.

If you **went** to see your grandmother she would be very pleased.
(= Why not go and see her?)
You might save enough money for a bike **if** you **got** a part-time job.
(= Why not get a part-time job?)
You could afford a bike **if** you **didn't spend** so much on clothes.
(= Stop spending so much on clothes)

3. Höfliche Vorschläge.
If + simple past hat keinen solchen starken Aufforderungscharakter wie *if + simple present.*

!

If you ring her tomorrow she will be very pleased.
You might ..... if you get a part-time job.
You will be able to afford ..... if you don't spend .....

I would be grateful **if** you **would send** me/**could let** me have some information about hotels in Great Britain.

4. Für formelle Bitten, z. B. in offiziellen Briefen:
if + would/could.

If everyone **would give** just a little money we could help the poor.
Jeff told Ann that **if** she **wouldn't help** him he wouldn't lend her any more records.

5. *If + would*:
Wenn *would* nach *if* steht, drückt es meistens eine Bereitschaft oder mangelnde Bereitschaft aus.

Die nachfolgenden Übungen helfen Ihnen, diese Regeln richtig anzuwenden.

Übung 6

Look at these pairs of sentences.

1. a) Would you go out with Ann if she asked you?
   b) Will you go out with Ann if she asks you?
2. a) Helen will go to America if she can save enough money.
   b) Helen would go to America if she could save enough money.
3. a) If Ken gets up early he won't be late for school
   b) If Ken got up early he wouldn't be late for school.

In welchen der obigen Sätze glaubt man eher, daß die Ereignisse des if-Satzes eintreten könnten?
In welchen Sätzen ist man sich nicht so sicher?

Übung 7

Put the following two lists together.

If Joe passes the exam	she wouldn't be late.
If Joe passed the exam	we wouldn't be able to change money.
If the bank closes at three	we could have a picnic.
If the bank closed at three	his teachers will be very surprised.
If Harry gives Ann a lift	we won't be able to change money.
If Harry gave Ann a lift	we can have a picnic.
If the weather is fine	his teachers would be very surprised.
If the weather were fine	she won't be late.

Übung 8

Look at this situation:
Diane thinks Carol should phone her brother, but Carol doesn't have his new phone number.
Carol says, <u>'I'd phone him if I had his new number.'</u> (phone/have)

Make similar sentences with 'if' + simple past.

1. Brian wants Eric to go to a football match with him, but Eric has to work.
   He says, ' . . . . ' (come/not have to)
2. Jill has seen a second-hand scooter that she would like to buy. But it is too expensive for her.
   She says, ' . . . . so expensive.' (buy/not be)
3. Ann has been offered a job, but they don't want to pay her very much.
   She tells the manager, 'I . . . . . if you . . . . . more.' (take/pay)
   Then she goes home and tells her mother, 'If they . . . . . I . . . . .' (give/take)
4. Derek is unhappy because he is so fat. But he eats a lot of cake. He says to his friend, 'If only I . . . . . so fat.' (not/be)
   His friend answers, 'If you . . . . . less cake you . . . . . .' (eat/not/be)
5. Mary is always tired. Steve thinks she goes to bed too late.
   He says, 'If you . . . . . so late all the time you . . . . . .' (not/go to bed/not/be)

§5 If-Sätze vom Typ III: nicht mehr erfüllbare Bedingungen

Typ III: If I **had done** A, then B **would/could ... have happened.**

a) **If** I **had known** you were ill I **would have come** to see you.
'**If** the car **hadn't broken down** we **would have gone** on holiday yesterday.' 'Where **would** you have gone?'

b) If Paul **hadn't drunk** so much last night he **wouldn't have** a headache now.
'What **would** you **be doing** now **if** I **hadn't come** to see you?' '**I'd** probably **be watching** TV.'

c) **If** I **hadn't broken** my leg I **would go skiing** with you next week.

1. Die Bedingungen sind nicht erfüllt und können auch nicht mehr erfüllt werden, weil sie sich auf die Vergangenheit beziehen. Sätze dieser Art dienen oft als Erklärungen.

Die Zeiten des Hauptsatzes ändern sich je nachdem, ob sie sich auf die Vergangenheit (a), Gegenwart (b) oder Zukunft (c) beziehen.

!

Would (have) erscheint fast nie im *if*-Satz (vgl. §4.4+5):
If I had known you were ill .....
(Nicht: * If I would have known .....).

Ben walked past me **as if** he **had never seen** me before.
If only I **hadn't taken** Sue's advice.

2. *If*-Sätze dieser Art können auch durch *as if* und *if only* eingeleitet werden.

Prüfen Sie nun bitte nach, ob Sie die verschiedenen *if*-Sätze richtig anwenden können.

Übung 9

Look at this conversation:

'I wouldn't have done it like that.' (How ... you)
'How would you have done it, then?'

Make similar replies.

1. 'I wouldn't have paid as much as that.' (How much ..... you)
2. 'You shouldn't have said that.' (What ..... you)
3. 'I wouldn't have gone there.' (Where ..... you)
4. 'You shouldn't have gone on a Saturday.' (When ..... you)

Übung 10

Complete the sentences by using the information in the two lists.

Something happened	The effect
Joanne went to a party.	She was late for work this morning.
Barbara went outside with wet hair.	She caught cold.
Frank lent Norman some money.	Norman could buy the bike.
Nobody told me Mr Jones was ill.	I didn't go to see him.
We brought a map.	We know where to go now.
Tony looked at a pretty girl.	He ran into a lorry.
Maria reminded Jeff about Ann's birthday.	He didn't forget it.
Sue didn't let Pete know she was coming.	He couldn't meet her at the station.
Caroline stayed up all night.	She is tired today.
Trevor lost his car keys.	We had to go by bus.
The Marsdens told us about this hotel.	We are staying here this week.
Derek didn't work hard	He didn't pass the exam.

Example: If Joanne hadn't gone to a party she wouldn't have been late for work this morning.

Übung 11

Which of these statements might have been made by

a) a good pupil before an exam b) a lazy pupil before an exam c) an ex-pupil?

1. 'If I worked harder I would probably pass.' .....
2. 'If I had worked harder I would have passed.' .....
3. 'If I work harder I should pass.' .....
4. 'If only I had worked harder.' .....

Übung 12

Which of these statements might have been made by

a) someone who is just learning to drive b) a bad driver c) someone who has just had an accident?

1. 'If I had driven more carefully I wouldn't have had an accident.'
2. 'If I drive carefully I won't have any accidents.'
3. 'If I were a better driver I wouldn't have so many accidents.'

Übung 13

Complete these sentences by using the correct forms of the verbs in brackets.

1. If the motor bike ..... so expensive Kate would buy it. (not/be)
2. If the bike ..... so expensive Kate would have bought it. (not/be)
3. You would be stupid if you ..... the job. (not/take) If I ..... you I would accept it. (be)
4. Debbie wouldn't go to New York even if she ..... the money. (have)
5. Debbie wouldn't have gone to New York even if she ..... the money. (have)
6. Alan would have been upset if we ..... him. (not/invite)
7. Alan will be upset if we ..... him. (not/invite)
8. Alan would be upset if we ..... him. (not/invite)
9. If Angela ..... her arm she would be playing in the team today. (not/break)
10. If Angela hadn't broken her arm she ..... last Saturday. (play)
11. If I ..... to drive a car I won't have to wait for buses all the time. (learn)
12. If I ..... a car I wouldn't have to wait for buses all the time. (can/drive)

10. Comparison of adjectives

Im Englischen gibt es viele Möglichkeiten, Vergleiche auszudrücken.
Einige Beispiele:

It's cheap**er** by bus
Cars are nois**ier than** bikes.
I'm **the** old**est** in the class.

Trains are **more expensive than** buses.
That's **the most exciting** film I've ever seen.

Your hands are **as** cold **as** ice.
My English is getting **better and better.**
The longer you stay up, **the more tired** you will be.

Prüfen Sie jetzt bitte nach, ob Sie diese verschiedenen Vergleichsformen richtig anwenden können.

Überprüfen Sie Ihr Wissen

Test 1

Um Vergleiche auszudrücken, braucht man die Komparativ- und Superlativformen von Adjektiven. Kennen Sie diese Formen?
Nennen Sie die Komparativ- und Superlativformen von folgenden Adjektiven:

a) tall	e) big	i) short	m) easy
b) clever	f) simple	j) interesting	n) thin
c) bad	g) good	k) fat	o) modern
d) expensive	h) ill	l) much	p) many

Diese Adjektive sind Beispiele für drei verschiedene Steigerungsformen.
Erkennen Sie die drei Gruppen?
War das schwierig? Wenn ja, sollten Sie sich § 1.1 und § 1.2. anschauen, bevor Sie weitermachen.

Test 2

Complete each sentence so that it means the same as the one before.

1. No one I know is more intelligent than you.
   You are ..... person I know.
2. Riding a bike is not as difficult as driving a car.
   Driving a car is ..... riding a bike. (difficult)
3. A bike is not as fast as a car.
   Cars are ..... bikes.
4. Germany is warmer than Scotland.
   Scotland isn't ..... Germany.
5. These shoes are too small.
   I need a ..... size. (big)
6. You hardly ever write to me.
   Please write a bit ..... (often)
7. If you practise English more you will learn faster.
   ..... you practise, ... you will learn.
8. I prefer love stories to science fiction.
   Love stories are ..... science fiction. (good) They are ..... (romantic)
9. Finding a job is getting harder all the time.
   It's getting ..... and ..... to find a job.
10. No one has ever said such a nice thing to me.
    That's ..... thing anyone has ever said to me.
11. An increasing number of people are learning English.
    ..... and ..... people are learning English.
12. Health is important. So is money.
    Money is just ..... health.
13. I like it better here every day.
    ..... (long) I stay here, ... I like it.

Grammatikregeln und Übungen

§1 Die regelmäßigen Steigerungsformen: Komparativ und Superlativ

a) tall – taller – the tallest
Let's go by bus. It's cheap**er.**
I'm **the** old**est** in the class.
b) simple – simpler – the simplest
Which is easi**er?** English or Maths?
I'm **the** clever**est** person in our school.

1. Mit -er, -est gesteigert werden
   a) einsilbige Adjektive:
   cheap, long, old, tall, short etc.
   b) zweisilbige Adjektive, die auf -er, -le, -ly, -ow, -y enden:
   clever, simple, lively, narrow, happy

!

In Großbritannien wächst die Tendenz, auch ein- und zweisilbige Adjektive mit *more* und *most* zu steigern, d.h. *more cheap, more clever* usw

difficult – more difficult – the most difficult
Geography is interesting.
Music is **more interesting.**
That's **the most exciting** film I've ever seen.

2. Mit *more* und *most* gesteigert werden zwei- und mehrsilbige Adjektive:
   boring, expensive, fashionable, modern, private, serious, useful etc.

§2 Die unregelmäßigen Steigerungsformen: Komparativ und Superlativ

I was **ill** yesterday, but today I'm much **better.**
That's the **worst** book I've ever read.
There aren't **many** sweets left. Have you got any **more?**

Unregelmäßig gesteigert werden:
good, bad, ill, much, many, little.

good	better	best
bad ill	worse	worst
much many	more	most
little	less	least

!

Man fragt *Which do you like best?* auch dann, wenn es sich nur um zwei Sachen handelt.

Übung 1

Complete this cartoon by using the superlative form of the opposite of 'heavy'.

I usually hold this one up
for the proud father,
it's the .....

§3 Vergleiche mit than, (not) as ..... as, (bigg)er and (bigg)er, the (soon)er ..... the (bett)er

I'm tall**er than** you. It's cheap**er** by bus **than** by train. Trains are **more expensive than** buses.	1. Zum Ausdruck eines höheren Grades: *-er than, more than*
Your hands are **as** cold **as** ice.	2. Zum Ausdruck des gleichen Grades: *as ..... as*
Your hair is**n't as** long **as** mine.	3. Zum Ausdruck eines geringeren Grades: *not as ..... as*
My English is getting bett**er and** bett**er.** The world is becoming a **more and more** dangerous place to live in.	4. Zum Ausdruck einer stetigen Steigerung: *(bigg)er and (bigg)er, more and more (interesting)* (immer interessanter)
The soon**er** we get home **the** bett**er.** **The more** difficult a problem is, **the more** interesting it is. **The** long**er** you stay up, **the more** tired you will be.	5. Zum Ausdruck einer proportionalen Steigerung: *the + -er/more ..... the + -er/more .....* (je ..... desto .....).

Übung 2

Put the adjectives into the comparative form.

1. Can you come . . . .? (early)
2. The . . . . . I get, the . . . . . I am. (old, happy)
3. I think you're . . . . . than the last time we met. (thin)
4. Can't you drive any . . . . .? (fast)
5. You're . . . . . at English than I am. (good)
6. English is getting . . . . . and . . . . . interesting for me. (much)
7. The . . . . . people who come on the trip, the . . . . . it will be. (many, cheap)

What is noisier than a jet? Two jets

Übung 3

Use comparative or superlative forms of the adjectives in brackets.

1. . . . . . of the people in our class are older than me. (much)
2. 'Is your toothache better?' 'No, it's . . . . .. (bad)
3. The . . . . . way to the station is through the park. (good)
4. If you need any . . . . . help give me a ring. (much)
5. That is the . . . . . mistake I have ever made. (bad)
6. Who is the . . . . . intelligent person you know? (much)
7. If you won't drive me home, the . . . . . you can do is lend me the bus fare. (little)

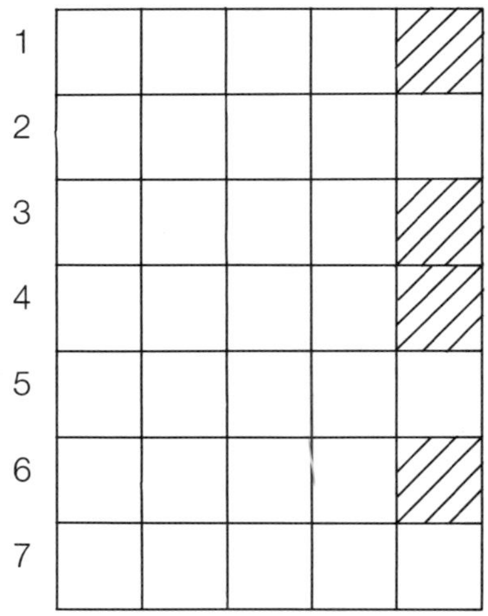

Übung 4

Complete these sentences so that each one means the same as the one above it.

Example:
John's dog is seven. So is Tina's.
John's dog is as old as Tina's.

1. Linda is 1.50 m tall. Alan is 1.20 m.
   Linda is . . . . . Alan. (tall)
   Alan is . . . . . Linda. (short)
2. English is easy. So is Maths.
   English is just . . . . . Maths. (easy.)

3. English is easy. Chemistry is more difficult.
   English is . . . . . chemistry. (difficult)
   Chemistry is . . . . . English. (difficult)
4. English is useful. Maths is useful, too.
   English is just . . . . . Maths. (useful)
5. Athens is about 27 °C in the summer, Madrid is about 25 °C.
   Madrid is . . . . . Athens. (hot)
   Athens is . . . . . Madrid. (hot)
6. About 3 million people live in Los Angeles; about 720,000 in San Francisco.
   Los Angeles is . . . . . San Francisco. (big)
   San Francisco is . . . . . Los Angeles. (big)
   There are . . . . . people in Los Angeles . . . . . in San Francisco. (more)
   There are . . . . . people in San Francisco . . . . . in Los Angeles. (many)
7. The Andes are 7,000 m high, the Rockies 4,500 m and the Atlas Mountains 4,000 m.
   The Andes are . . . . . (high)
   The Rockies are . . . . . the Atlas Mountains. (high)
   The Atlas Mountains are . . . . . the Rockies. (high)
8. The red sweater costs five pounds, the green one five pounds fifty and the yellow one seven pounds.
   The yellow one is . . . . . (expensive)
   The red one is . . . . . (cheap)
   The green one is . . . . . the red one. (expensive)
9. Which is earlier: eleven thirty-two or twenty-seven minutes to twelve?
   . . . . . is . . . . (early)
   . . . . . is . . . . (later)

Übung 5

What do you think? Write down some of your opinions:

1. Boxing, ice-hockey, handball, basketball, football, motor cycle racing . . .
   exciting, interesting, dangerous, safe . . .
   more . . . than; the most . . .; not as . . . as . . .; just as . . . as . . .; etc.

   Example:
   Motor cycle racing is more dangerous than ice-hockey. Basketball is the most interesting. Motor cycle racing is not as exciting as basketball etc.
2. Westerns, love stories, thrillers, science fiction stories, war stories . . .
   exciting, interesting, relaxing, entertaining . . .
3. Collecting stamps, watching television, playing the (piano . . .),
   cooking, sewing, knitting, doing woodwork, reading, dancing . . .
   exciting, boring, restful, difficult, easy, interesting . . .

11. Adverbs

In diesem Kapitel wiederholen wir alles, was Sie wissen müssen, um die verschiedenen Adverbien richtig anwenden zu können.

Zunächst einige Beispiele:

Wir brauchen **Adverbien**, um Details anzugeben.
Sie beantworten die Fragen: wann? wie?
wie oft? wie lange? bis zu welchem Grad? wo/wohin?
Sie können auch Einstellungen und Kommentare des Sprechers ausdrücken.

I got up **at seven o'clock.**
The bus travelled **slowly.**
Steve is **always** late.
Carol stayed in England **for three weeks.**
I was **very** nervous.
Let's go **home.**

Prüfen Sie nun nach, wieviel Sie schon können.

Überprüfen Sie Ihr Wissen

Test 1

Complete the following sentences by changing the adjectives in brackets into adverbs.

1. It is ..... cold today (awful)
2. Mrs Simmons is ..... ill. (critical)
3. It will ..... rain today. (probable)
4. Carol smiled at the new girl ..... (friendly)
5. The old man climbed the stairs ..... (difficult)
6. We got up very ..... this morning. (late)
7. Have you seen Helen .....? (late)
8. 'Margaret has been working very ..... all week.' (hard) 'That's ..... surprising, she's taking her exams next week.' (hard)
9. Your hair looks ..... (nice)

Test 2

Translate these sentences into English.

1. Es gibt einen Zug morgen nachmittag um zehn vor fünf.
2. Gehst du noch in die Schule?
3. Sue hat noch keine Arbeitsstelle gefunden. Wahrscheinlich findet sie auch keine vor Weihnachten.
4. Wir sind am Samstag in die Disco gegangen.
5. Mike spricht ganz gut Französisch. Angela auch.
6. Teresa steht immer früh auf.
7. Ich bin letzte Woche dreimal ins Kino gegangen.
8. Dieses Geschäft verkauft nur Schallplatten.
9. „Ich weiß nicht einmal Karins Telefonnummer.“ „Ich auch nicht.“
10. Ich kann Ihnen leider nicht helfen. Ich bin nämlich fremd hier. Ich habe jedoch einen Stadtplan. Vielleicht hilft er Ihnen.

Grammatikregeln und Übungen

§ 1 Arten der Adverbien

Man unterscheidet zwischen:

I got up **at seven o'clock**

1. Adverbien der Zeit *(adverbs of time): this morning, yesterday, at five o'clock, before lunch, for . . ., since . . .* etc. (→ § 3)

I caught the bus **round the corner.**

2. Adverbien des Ortes/der Richtung *(adverbs of place): at home, on the bus, under the table, outside, to school, into* etc. (→ § 4)

The bus travelled very **slowly.**

3. Adverbien der Art und Weise *(adverbs of manner): slowly, carefully, in a friendly way, with difficulty* etc. (→ § 5)

The journey **usually** takes twenty minutes.

4. Häufigkeitsadverbien *(adverbs of frequency)*: sometimes, often, always, usually, never etc. (→ § 6)

I was **very** nervous when I finally arrived for the interview.

5. Adverbien des Grades *(adverbs of degree): very, completely, fairly, quite, pretty, too, enough, almost, a bit* etc. (→ § 7)

'I **only** had a sandwich for lunch.' 'I didn't have much **either.**'

6. Hervorhebende Adverbien *(focusing adverbs): also, even, only, especially, mainly, either . . . or, neither . . . nor* etc. (→ § 8)

Luckily, my new boss was a very understanding woman.

7. Satzadverbien *(sentence adverbs): naturally, luckily, unfortunately, maybe, anyway* etc. (→ § 9)

§2 Die Bildung von Adverbien

Anders als im Deutschen unterscheiden sich die meisten englischen Adverbien von Adjektiven der Form nach:

Adjektiv	Adverb
a slow car	he drove slow**ly**

Es gibt einige Regeln, die man bei der Bildung von englischen Adverbien beachten muß:

intelligent – intelligent**ly**
clear – clear**ly**

1. Die meisten Adverbien werden von Adjektiven abgeleitet, indem man '-ly' anfügt.

What a **lovely** dress!
She is very **friendly.**

2. Vorsicht bei Adjektiven, die auf '-ly' enden! An diese Adjektive wird kein '-ly' angehängt. Sie werden oft mit *way* umschrieben: *in a lively, silly, kindly way*

I got up **early.** (adv.)
I took an **early** train. (adj.)
I work **hard.** (adv.)
This chair is **hard.** (adj.)
You speak English **well.** (adv.: „gut")
I am not very **well** (adj.: „gesund")

3.a) Einige Adverbien haben die gleiche Form wie das entsprechende Adjektiv: *fast, high, low, deep, near, far, late, long, daily, weekly, early, hard.*

3.b) Einige Adverbien und Adjektive haben bei gleicher Form verschiedene Bedeutungen.

Susan works **hard.**
Susan **hardly** works.
The plane is flying **high.**
This book is **highly** interesting.

Adj.	
hard (= hart)	hard (= hart)
	hardly (= kaum)
high (= hoch)	highly (= sehr)
short (= kurz)	shortly (= bald)
near (= nah)	nearly (= beinahe)
late (= spät)	lately (= vor kurzem)

4. Manche Adverbien haben eine andere Bedeutung als die Adjektive, von denen sie ursprünglich abgeleitet wurden.

These shoes feel comfortable.
(= **are** comfortable)

This tastes awful.
(= **is** awful)

The answer is correct.

5. Nach den Verben *be, look, feel, seem, smell, sound, taste* steht, da es sich ja nicht um eine Tätigkeit handelt, ein Adjektiv.

!

She looked serious.
(Adj.: Sie sah ernst aus.)

She looked at me seriously.
(Adv.: Sie sah mich ernst an.)

I feel good. (Adj.: wohl)
I feel well. (Adj.: gesund)

Übung 1

Complete these sentences by forming adverbs from the adjectives in brackets.

1. The film will ..... be over before eleven. (probable)
2. 'Do you think we'll be able to get tickets?' '.....' (hopeful)
3. Neil looks very ..... today. (cheerful) He is smiling ..... to himself. (happy)
4. Alan plays the guitar very ...... (good)
5. Jill couldn't stay ....., she was in a hurry. (long)
6. That woman must be ..... rich. Have you ever seen her car? (fantastic)
7. The magazine 'Punch' appears ..... (weekly)
8. You are ..... right. (absolute)
9. 'If we set off ..... we'll get there on time.' (early) 'Yes, but don't drive too .....' (fast)
10. Carol smiled at the new girl ...... (friendly)
11. Grandfather climbed the stairs ...... (difficult)
12. 'What are you cooking? It smells .....' (good) 'Yes, it tastes quite ....., too.' (nice)

Übung 2

Translate these sentences into English.

1. Harry und Ken haben sich geprügelt. Harry hat Ken sehr hart geschlagen.
2. Kannst Du etwas lauter reden, bitte. Ich kann Dich kaum hören.
3. Helen wohnt in der Nähe vom Bahnhof.
4. Gestern habe ich beinahe meinen Bus verpaßt.
5. Dieser Turm ist sehr hoch.
6. Dieses Buch ist höchst interessant.
7. Heute abend komme ich spät nach Hause.
8. Hast Du Barbara in letzter Zeit gesehen?

Which rule helped you? § .....

§3 Adverbien der Zeit (adverbs of time)

Diese Adverbien beantworten die Frage „wann?“, „(für) wie lange?“, „wie oft?“. Sie stehen:

We're going to a disco **tomorrow night.**
Don't do that **again.**
Carol stayed in England **for three weeks.**

1. Meistens am Satzende, besonders:
again, late, now, these days, then, today, this (morning), yesterday (afternoon), two months ago, for . . ., since . . . etc.

We're going to have a lot of fun today: **first** we'll go to the fair, **then** we'll see a film and **afterwards** we'll go to a party.

2. Am Anfang eines Satzes oder Nebensatzes, wenn sie hervorgehoben werden oder zur Gegenüberstellung, besonders:
afterwards, earlier, eventually, finally, first, immediately, lately, next, once, soon.

Tony has to be home **by ten** on weekdays.
I was born **at midnight** on New Year's Day in 1973.

3. Bei mehreren adverbialen Bestimmungen ist die Reihenfolge:
genauere Angabe + weniger genaue
at midnight – on New Year's Day – in 1973

4. *Still*: etwas dauert länger als erwartet (noch immer).
Still steht

bei bejahten Sätzen und Fragen:

a) I **still love** you.
b) Jill **is still** in bed.
c) Do you **still collect** stamps?

a) *still* + Verb
b) *be* + *still*
c) hat das Verb mehrere Teile, so bleibt die Reihenfolge:
still + Vollverb

bei verneinten Sätzen:

d) The letter **has still not** come.

d) Hilfsverb + *still* + *not*
Um *still* hervorzuheben, kann man die Reihenfolge ändern:

e) The letter **still has not** come.

e) *still* + Hilfsverb + *not*

Is Sandra back **yet?**
Sandra isn't back **yet.**

5. *Yet*: Erkundigungen, ob etwas eingetreten ist (schon) und verneinten Antworten darauf (noch nicht).
Stellung: Satzende.

! Is Sandra back already?
(= Verwunderung ausdrücken)

Übung 3:

Put these sentences in the correct order and say which rules helped you.

1. on Fridays/doesn't close/the shop/until six
   The shop . . . .
2. by about eleven/home/should be/we
   We . . . .
3. on Saturday nights/go out/I/with my friends.
   I/on Sundays/but/with my parents/go out
   I . . . .
   . . . . with my parents.
4. in August/going/on holiday/we're.
   to see me/my penfriend/is coming/in September
   We're . . . . to see me.
5. open/still/the shop/is
   The shop . . . .
6. I/to school/go/still
   . . . .
7. haven't met/yet/my penfriend/I
   I . . . .
8. play/you/still/the guitar/do/?
   . . . . the guitar?

§4 Adverbien des Ortes/der Richtung (adverbs of place)

Diese Adverbien beantworten die Fragen „wo?“ und „wohin?“. Sie stehen:

Can you meet me **at the station?**
Mary wants to visit a friend **in hospital.**
It's cold **outside.**

1. Am Satzende.

At the station there was a huge crowd of people.
Here comes the bride.
There's Dennis. I wonder where he's going.

2. Am Satzanfang, wenn sie besonders hervorgehoben werden.
   Here und *there* stehen oft am Anfang.

a) The town hall is **in the Market Square in the town centre.**

b) We went **to the cinema last night.**
Let's go **home early.**
We'll meet **at the bus stop tonight.**
I have been going **to school for ten years.**

c) We'll meet **tonight at the bus stop opposite our house.**
We'll meet **in town at the pub near the town hall.**

3. Treffen mehrere Adverbien zusammen, gilt folgende Reihenfolge:
   a) genauere Angabe + weniger genaue
   b) Ort/Richtung + Zeit

   O(rt) vor Z(eit)
   im Alphabet

   c) kurz + lang

Übung 4

Der Mann am Fenster sagt auf Deutsch:
„Das da drüben ist das Empire State Building."
What is he saying in English?

Übung 5

Translate these sentences into English and say which rule helped you.

1. Meine Großeltern wohnen in einem kleinen Haus auf dem Lande.
2. Ich wurde 1973 in einem kleinen Dorf im Süden geboren.
3. In Deutschland trinkt man viel Kaffee. In Großbritannien trinkt man mehr Tee.
4. Wir fahren im Juli nach Frankreich.
5. Der Zug kommt um sieben Uhr achtundvierzig in Paris an.

Übung 6

Neil had a busy time last week. Write down all the things he did. Start each sentence with 'He .....'.

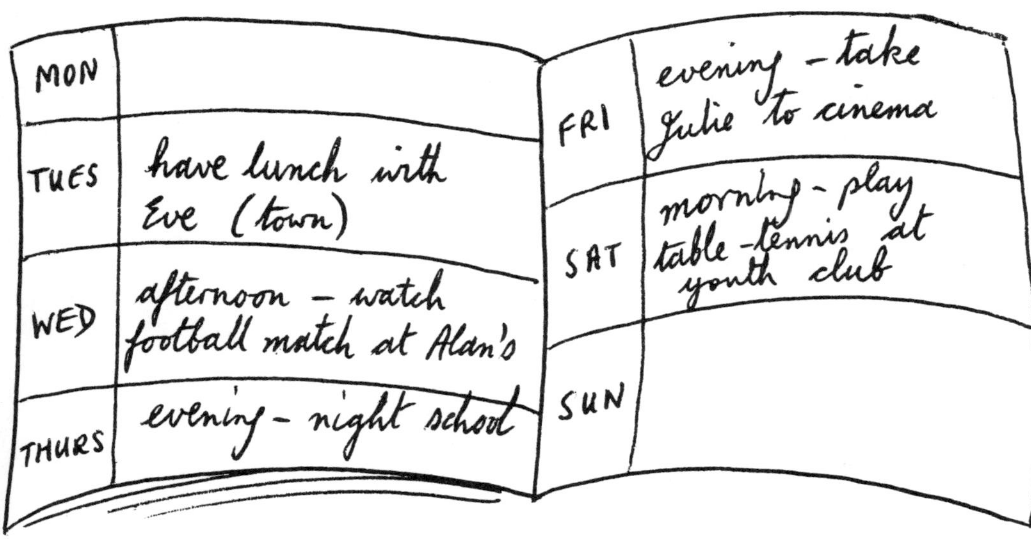

§5 Adverbien der Art und Weise (adverbs of manner)

Diese Adverbien beantworten die Frage „wie?“ (auf welche Art und Weise?).

Sie stehen:

You speak English very **well.**
Dora opened the letter **slowly.**

1. Normalerweise am Satzende.

Dora **slowly** opened the letter.

2. Zur Hervorhebung werden manche Adverbien, z. B. *quickly, slowly, carefully*, vor das Verb gestellt.

!
Im Gegensatz zum Deutschen erscheint das Adverb im Englischen nicht zwischen Verb und Objekt:
Dora öffnete langsam den Brief.

Suddenly there was a crash.
Luckily, no one was hurt.

3. Um eine dramatische Wirkung zu erzielen, werden manche Adverbien an den Satzanfang gestellt. (Vgl. §9).

Steven read the article **carefully** and **with great interest.**

Mrs Davies sat **quietly in her armchair every evening.**

Every evening Mrs Davies sat **quietly in her armchair.**

4. Treffen mehrere Adverbien zusammen, gilt folgende Reihenfolge:
   a) zwei Adverbien der Art und Weise:
      kurz + lang
   b) Art u. Weise + Ort/Richtung + Zeit
      A vor O vor Z

Um eine Anhäufung zu vermeiden, wird die Zeitbestimmung oft an den Satzanfang gestellt.

§6 Adverbien der Häufigkeit (adverbs of frequency)

Diese Adverbien geben darüber Auskunft, wie oft und ob überhaupt etwas passiert bzw. passiert ist.
Sie stehen:

Steve **is always** late.	1. *Be* + Adverb
Steve **always comes** late. Alan has **never danced** with a girl. Have you **ever driven** a car? I **usually have to** wait for Steve.	2. Adverb + Vollverb. In dieser Stellung stehen meistens *always, often, usually, sometimes, never.* **!** Im Deutschen ist die Reihenfolge umgekehrt: Steve kommt immer zu spät. **!** *Have to* wird als Teil des Vollverbs angesehen, deshalb steht die adverbiale Bestimmung vor *have to*.
Never drink when you're driving. **Usually** I get up early, **but** today I was late.	3. Wenn das Adverb besonders hervorgehoben werden soll, steht es am Anfang des Satzes (oft in Verbindung mit *but* oder *(al)though*.
We have English **three times a week.** I have only met Derek **once.**	4. Einige Häufigkeitsadverbien stehen normalerweise am Satzende: *once, again and again, a few times, now and then, now and again, (twice) a (day).*
Marion went **to London twice.** Marion went **to London twice last year.**	5. Treffen mehrere Adverbien zusammen, so gilt folgende Reihenfolge: a) Ort/Richtung + Häufigkeit b) Ort/Richtung + Häufigkeit + Zeit

§7 Adverbien des Grades (adverbs of degree)

Diese Adverbien beantworten die Frage „bis zu welchem Grad?“. Sie dienen auch zur Verstärkung einer Aussage.
Sie stehen:

Brian is **very** ill.
I **completely** forgot to post your letter.

1. Vor dem Wort, das sie näher bestimmen: *quite, very, really, completely, hardly, almost, a bit, too, enough*

It's **quite a** long way.
I **quite** like this record.

! *quite* steht vor *a(n)*

I don't **really think** so.
It will **probably rain** tomorrow.

2. Bei Verben mit mehreren Teilen (*don't ..... think, will ..... rain):*
Adverb + Vollverb

Jeff **probably won't** come.

! In verneinten Sätzen steht *probably* vor dem Hilfsverb.

Turn the radio down **a bit**, please.
I don't like that music **much.**

3. *Much, a lot, a bit, a little* stehen am Satzende, wenn sie ein Verb näher bestimmen.

Übung 7

Translate these sentences into English.

1. Deine Mutter spielt erstaunlich gut Tischtennis.
2. Jennifer zeigte uns stolz ihre Briefmarkensammlung.
3. Der Sportlehrer erklärte sorgfältig die Spielregeln.
4. Janet zog schnell ihren Mantel an und eilte aus dem Haus.
5. Unser Nachbar kickte wütend unseren Ball aus seinem Garten.

Auf welche Regel muß man besonders achten?:
Im Englischen darf das Adverb ..... zwischen ..... und ..... stehen (§ .....).

Übung 8

Answer these questions about yourself, using 'I always/sometimes/usually, never .....'.

1. When do you go to bed on weekdays?
2. When do you get up in the week?
3. What do you do in the evenings on weekdays?
4. What do you do on Saturday nights?
5. Is there anything you never do?

Which rule helped you? § .....

Übung 9

Make complete sentences, using the adverb in brackets. Write down the rule which helped you.

1. The Donalds/have lived/in the country (always)
2. We/have sports (once a week)
3. Susan/has been/to a pop concert (never)
4. Derek/has been out/with Linda (a few times)
5. I/have to/tell my parents/where I'm going (always)
6. I/can remember/that girl's name (never)

Übung 10

Choose a word from each box to complete these sentences. Only use each word once. Always start with the first box.

~~awfully~~	probably	seriously
completely	quite	terribly
nearly	quite a	very
probably	really	

be	ill	nice
changed	interesting	sorry
cheap	know	won't be able
~~hot~~	missed	

Example:
It's awfully hot in here. Can we open a window?

1. Brian's mother is .... in hospital.
2. Don .... the train, he got up so late.
3. I'm .... I broke your record.
4. These records are .... They're less than a pound.
5. I .... to go on holiday this year. I haven't enough money.
6. When Sally went back to the village where she was born everything had .... She hardly recognised it.
7. Diane is .... person. She's .... to talk to.
8. 'What time are you coming home?' 'I don't ...., but I'll .... late.'

§8 Hervorhebende Adverbien (focusing adverbs)

Diese Adverbien heben einen Teil des Satzes hervor.

Sie stehen:

I like sports, **especially football**. I **especially like** swimming. Diane goes swimming and she **also plays** hockey.	1. Meistens vor dem Ausdruck, den sie näher bestimmen, besonders: *also, especially, even, just, mainly, mostly, only.*
We **are just** good friends.	2. *Be* + Adverb
I don't **particularly like** swimming. Eric can't **even boil** an egg.	3. Bei Verben mit mehreren Teilen: Adverb + Vollverb
'I like classical music.' – 'I do, **too**. But I like pop **as well**.' 'I don't like classical music and I don't like pop **either**.' 'Andy doesn't like **either** pop **or** classical music.' – 'Well, I don't **either**.'	4. *'Too, as well, either'* stehen am Satzende.
Neither of the films look particularly interesting: **neither** the western **nor** the love story.	5. *Neither ..... nor* stehen immer am Anfang.

Das war doch ganz einfach, oder nicht? Mal sehen .....

Übung 11

Translate these sentences into English.

1. Ich gehe nur einkaufen. Ich komme gleich wieder.
2. Wir sind nur eine Stunde im Konzert geblieben. Wir konnten nicht einmal Sitzplätze bekommen.
3. Sue liest Comics. Sie liest aber auch Zeitungen.
4. John kann am Wochenende nicht kommen. Mike kann auch nicht.
5. „Ich habe meine Hausaufgaben noch nicht gemacht." „Ich auch nicht."

§9 Satzadverbien (sentence adverbs)

Diese Adverbien beziehen sich auf den ganzen Satz. Sie drücken eine Einstellung oder einen Kommentar des Sprechers aus.
Sie stehen:

Honestly, I don't care what people think of me.
Obviously, you don't believe me.

1. Normalerweise am Anfang:
actually, anyway, hopefully, however, in fact, officially, maybe, of course, obviously, perhaps, surely, (un)fortunately, from (my/a) ..... point of view.

Bill has to go into hospital**, unfortunately.**

The operation**, however,** will not be a difficult one.

2. Manchmal am Satzende.

!

However steht oft in der Satzmitte und wird durch Kommas als Kommentar gekennzeichnet.

Übung 12

Translate the following sentences into English. Use adverbs to express the underlined words, but be careful where you put them.

1. Ich kann euch leider nicht am Bahnhof abholen.
2. Es gibt hier bestimmt eine Bank in der Nähe.
3. Hoffentlich kann ich im Sommer nach England.
4. Ob ich die Stelle bekomme hängt natürlich von meinen Prüfungsergebnissen ab.
5. Hast du übrigens Tony in letzter Zeit gesehen?
6. Sylvia hat vielleicht recht.
7. Im Grunde stimme ich Ihnen zu. Es gibt jedoch eine Schwierigkeit.
8. Der Unfall war glücklicherweise nicht so schlimm.
9. „Sollen wir zu dem Fußballspiel gehen?" – „Mir gefällt Fußball eigentlich gar nicht. Um ehrlich zu sein, ich hasse es." – „Ich persönlich habe auch kein großes Interesse an Fußball."

§ 10 Inversion

Manchmal wird eine adverbiale Bestimmung besonders hervorgehoben, um eine dramatische Wirkung zu erzielen.

Never had I seen such a crowd.
Not only did he take us all out, he also paid for the meal.
Under no circumstances are you to leave this room.

1. Hervorhebung des Adverbs (meistens nur in der geschriebenen Sprache) macht eine Inversion von Subjekt und Hilfsverb notwendig, vgl. die normale Stellung: I had never seen such a crowd.

   Adverbien, die eine solche Inversion notwendig machen:
   not only, hardly, no sooner ..... than, never, not until, under no circumstances, only

Übung 13

Rewrite the following by putting the underlined adverbs at the beginning of the sentence and making the necessary changes.

1. We had **hardly** gone to bed when there was a knock at the door.
2. Peter had **no sooner** arrived than he had to go again.
3. Doreen can **not only** play the piano, she is also a well-known folk singer.

Übung 14

Rewrite the sentences with underlined words in them, following rule § 10.

Mr and Mrs Gambols' niece and nephew have come to stay with them for a few days. But the children had no sooner arrived than they started running round the living-room. The boy fell down and put his foot through the television. He not only broke the set, but also his leg and arm and he hurt his head. Mrs Gambol had to fetch the doctor.
The doctor had hardly left when the little girl kicked a football through the window. She not only broke the window, she als cut her arm on some glass. It was not until the children were in bed that the Gambols could sit down and rest. "George," said Mrs Gambol, "you're not to invite those children again, under no circumstances."

§ 11 Englische Verben anstelle deutscher Adverbien

Viele deutsche Adverbien werden im Englischen nicht durch Adverbien, sondern durch Verben wiedergegeben.

It**'s getting** cold.
= Es wird **allmählich** kalt.
Susanne **tends to** make careless mistakes.
= Susanne macht **gerne** Leichtsinnsfehler.

Deutsche Adverbien → englische Verben:
andauernd – *go on/keep on*
anscheinend – *appear/seem*
allmählich – *get/grow*
bekanntlich – *as everyone knows*
früher – *used to*
gern – *tend to; like; prefer*
leider – *be afraid/sorry*
lieber – *prefer*
nämlich – *you know/you see*
offenbar – *appear/seem*
sicher – *be sure/certain*
vielleicht – *may/might*
vermutlich – *suppose*
weiter(hin) – *go on/keep on*
zufällig – *happen to*

Übung 15

Translate the following into English.

1. Lach' nicht andauernd.
2. Andy hat anscheinend eine neue Stelle.
3. Früher habe ich gerne Briefmarken gesammelt.
4. Heute mache ich lieber Sport in meiner Freizeit.
5. Tony hat die Fahrprüfung nicht bestanden, aber er sagt, er versucht es weiter. Vielleicht hat er das nächste Mal Glück.
6. Dieser Film wird allmählich langweilig.
7. Ich kann am Samstag leider nicht kommen.
8. Bist du sicher, daß der Zug um zehn ankommt? – Ja, aber er hat offenbar Verspätung.
9. Haben Sie zufällig eine Karte von London?
10. Es ist vermutlich billiger mit der Bahn zu fahren. Ich habe nämlich nicht viel Geld.

12. Indirect speech

Es gibt zwei Möglichkeiten, das, was man selbst oder was ein anderer gesagt hat, wiederzugeben:

a) durch Wiederholen der wörtlichen Rede, z. B.
'Don't drive too fast!'
Sue said, 'Don't drive too fast.'

b) durch **indirekte Rede.** Hier hat man verschiedene Möglichkeiten, sich auszudrücken, z. B.

direct speech	**indirect/reported speech**
Ann: 'I **know** what to do.'	Ann **said, 'I know what to do**.' Ann **says** she **knows** what to do. Ann **said** she **knows** what to do. Ann **said** she **knew** what to do.
Derek: 'I **went** to the cinema **last night**.'	Derek **told** me he **went** to the cinema **last night**. Derek **told** me he **went/(had gone)** to the cinema **the night before/on Monday**.
Neil: '**I** bought **this** sweater for **my** girl-friend.'	Neil **showed me a sweater** and **told** me he had bought **it** for **his** girlfriend.

Überprüfen Sie Ihr Wissen

Test

Complete these sentences.

1. Joe: 'I'm not coming to the party on Saturday.'
   Joe says he ..... coming to the party on Saturday.
2. Mike: 'What were you doing when I phoned?'
   Mike wanted to know what I ..... when he phoned.
3. Grandma: 'If I had known you were coming I would have made a cake.'
   Grandma said that if she ..... we were coming she ..... a cake.
4. Eric: 'If I knew Tony's number we could ring him.'
   Eric said that if he ..... Tony's number we could ring him.
5. Sue: 'I want to learn to drive.'
   a) Sue told me she ..... to learn to drive. She's having her first lesson next week.
   b) Sue told me she ..... to learn to drive, but I think she has changed her mind now.
6. Sue: 'I like Mike.'
   Sue told me that she ..... Mike.
7. Jill: 'I don't smoke.'
   Ben: 'Look, Jill's smoking! She told me that she ..... smoke.'
8. Jill: 'I had a bad dream last night.'
   a) Jill told me she ..... a bad dream last night.
   b) Jill told me she ..... a bad dream the night before.
9. Jeff: 'I don't know if I can help you.'
   a) Jeff said he didn't know if he ..... help us.
   b) Jeff said he didn't know if he ..... help us.
10. Neil: 'I bought this sweater for my girlfriend.'
    Neil told me he had bought ..... sweater for his girlfriend.
11. On Friday Chris says: 'It's my birthday tomorrow.'
    Last Friday Chris told me that it was his birthday .....
12. Diane: 'What shall I do?'
    Diane didn't know .....

Grammatikregeln und Übungen

§1 Die Funktionen der indirekten Rede

Die indirekte Rede kann für folgende Zwecke gebraucht werden:

'Don't drive tôo fast!'
– Sue **told** me not to/**said** I shouldn't drive too fast.

The Prime Minister **did not accept** the suggestion.

1. Für neutrale, distanzierte Berichte.
Die Aussage wird berichtet, ohne sich mit ihr zu identifizieren: man gibt keine Gewähr für die Richtigkeit; man gibt auch nicht zu erkennen, wie man selber dazu steht.

Linda to Ann: 'Switch that radio off.'
– Linda **politely asked/begged/ordered/warned** Ann to switch her radio off.

Sue: 'Don't drive too fast.'
– Sue **warned/advised** me not to drive too fast.

Prime Minister: 'That's absolute rubbish!'
– The Prime Minister **disapproved of/ completely rejected/laughed at** the suggestion.

2. Detailliertere bzw. subjektivere Berichte.
Der Berichterstatter muß auch die Art und den Ton der wörtlichen Rede wiedergeben, z. B. ob es sich um eine höfliche Bitte, einen Befehl, einen Ratschlag, eine Empfindung, Hoffnung, Befürchtung usw. handelt. Dabei kann die Aussage natürlich absichtlich gefärbt werden.
Häufige Verben:
advise, ask politely, complain, criticise, doubt, hope, order, promise, suggest, warn usw.

Ken: '**I'll lend** you £5.'
– Dave: 'Ken **said** he **would lend** me £5, but he hasn't done yet'.

3. Die indirekte Rede wird oft gebraucht, um auf Fehlinformationen, Widersprüche und nicht eingehaltene Versprechen hinzuweisen (§ 4.3)

Übung 1

Report the following statements

a) without adding your own opinion
b) with your own opinion added

Use the following words: say, tell, warn, order, shout (to), advise, promise, finally allow, complain

Example:
Keith to Ann: 'Don't drive so fast!'
a) Keith told Ann not to drive so fast.
b) Keith warned/advised Ann not to drive so fast.

1. Mike to Steve: 'I'll help you.'
a) Mike ..... he would .....
b) Mike ..... to help Steve.

2. Mr Reed to Ben: 'Get out of my garden!'
a) Mr Reed ..... to get ....
b) Mr Reed ..... to get ....

3. Frank: 'It's cold!'
a) Frank ..... was cold.
b) Frank ..... that ..... was cold.

4. Mrs Williams to her daughter: 'Don't go out without a coat.'
a) Mrs Williams ..... not to go ....
b) Mrs Williams ..... not to go ....

5. Mr Jennings to Sarah: 'Alright, you can go to the pop concert.'
a) ..... that Sarah could ....
b) ..... Sarah to go ....

Bei der Wiedergabe von wörtlicher Rede muß man manchmal einige Veränderungen vornehmen, manchmal nicht.

§2 Einleitendes Verb im Präsens

Joe: 'I**'ve failed** my exam.'

a) – Joe says he **has failed** his exam.
– Listen. Joe is telling Sue that he **has failed** his exam.

b) – Has Joe told you that he **has failed** his exam?

c) – Joe won't tell anyone that he **has failed** his exam.
– Joe will have told his girlfriend that he **has failed** his exam.

Wenn das einleitende Verb im
a) *present tense*
b) *present perfect*
c) *future*
steht, bleibt die Zeit der direkten Rede unverändert.

Übung 2

Write out these messages in full, then tell your friend what they mean.

Example:
Uncle George's telegram: ARRIVING SATURDAY
George: *'I'm arriving on Saturday.'*
You to friend: *Uncle George says he's arriving on Saturday.*

1. Steve's telegram: LOST PASSPORT
Steve: 'I've . . . .'
You to friend: Steve says he . . . .

2. Mary's telegram: MONEY STOLEN
Mary: 'My . . . . . has . . . .'
You to friend: Mary says her . . . .

3. Martin's note: Going to cinema tonight. Go with me?
Martin: 'I . . . . . tonight. Do you want . . . . .?'
You to friend: Martin says . . . . . tonight.
He asks if we . . . . . him.

4. Derek's note: Rang you yesterday. Weren't in. Call in tonight.
Derek: 'I . . . . . you yesterday, but . . . . . .
'll . . . . .'
You to friend: Derek says . . . . . me yesterday, but . . . . . He says he . . . . .

§3 Einleitendes Verb im simple past oder past continuous: keine Veränderung der direkten Rede

a) Mike: 'What **were** you **doing** when I phoned?'
– Mike wanted to know what I **was doing** when he phoned.
(Not: 'had been doing')

b) Grandma: 'If I **had known** you were coming I **would have made** a cake.'
– Grandma explained that if she **had known** we were coming she **would have made** a cake.

c) Janet: 'I **would go** to England with you if I **could.'**
– Janet was saying that she **would go** to England with us if she **could.**

1. In folgenden Fällen bleibt die Zeit der direkten Rede unverändert:

Die wörtliche Rede steht im
a) *past continuous*
b) *past perfect*
c) *conditional*
d) *conditional perfect*

(Das *past continuous* kann zu *past perfect continuous* verändert werden; das ist aber höchst selten).

Eric: '**If** I **knew** Tony's phone number we could ring him.'
– Eric said that if he **knew** Tony's number we could ring him.

Carol: 'I **wish** the exams **were** over.'
– Carol said she wished the exams **were** over.

2. Das *simple past* in irrealen Bedingungs- und Wunschsätzen wird beim Berichten nicht verändert.

Mr Thatcher: 'I **was involved** in the deal ..... I **met** my mother .....'
– Mr Thatcher admitted (.....) that he **was involved** in the 1981 deal and **met** his mother during her official visit to Oman. (Observer, 15. 2. 84)

3. Das *simple past* der wörtlichen Rede bleibt häufig unverändert, besonders dann, wenn der in der wörtlichen Rede ausgedrückte Zustand bzw. Vorgang nicht so lange her ist.

a) Sue: 'I **want** to learn to drive.'
① Sue told me she **wants** to learn to drive. (= she still wants to)
② Vgl. Sue told me she **wanted** to learn to drive. (= I don't know if she still wants to)

b) Jean: 'My boyfriend **is working** in York.'
① Jean told me that her boyfriend **is working** in York. (= he still is)
② ('. . . . . **was working** . . . . .' (= I don't know if he still is)

c) Eric: 'Carol **has bought** a moped.'
① Eric was telling me that Carol **has bought** a moped. (= I believe him)
② '. . . . . **had bought** . . . . .' (= I'm not sure if that is true)

d) Ann: 'Jeff **is having** a party tonight!'
① Ann said that Jeff **is having** a party. (= I believe he will)
② '. . . . . **was having** . . . . .' (= I'm not sure if he really will)

4. In den folgenden Fällen kann, muß sich aber nichts ändern.
Die wörtliche Rede steht im
a) *simple present*
b) *present continuous*
c) *present perfect*
d) *future*

Die Zeiten bleiben erhalten, wenn die Aussage zum Zeitpunkt des Berichtens noch zutrifft bzw. bevorsteht. (Vgl. § 4,1)

!

Wenn die oben genannten Zeiten bei der Wiedergabe in der indirekten Rede verändert werden, bedeutet es meistens, daß der Berichtende an der Aussage zweifelt. (Vgl. § 4,3)

Sue: 'I **like** Mike.'
– Sue told me that she **likes/liked** Mike.

My penfriend: '**Is** Alan British?'
– My penfriend wanted to know if you **are/were** British.

5. Für Allgemeingültiges kann sowohl das *simple present* als auch das *simple past* gebraucht werden. Es ist kaum ein Bedeutungsunterschied.

Das sieht zunächst vielleicht etwas verwirrend aus. Aber nur keine Angst! Die nächsten Übungen helfen Ihnen, Fehler zu vermeiden.

Übung 3

Complete these sentences by reporting what someone else said. Write down the numbers of the rules which helped you.

1. Brenda: 'Sometimes I wish I had a part-time job.'
   Brenda told me that she sometimes wishes she ..... a part-time job.
2. Elaine: 'I was listening to records this afternoon, so I didn't hear the phone.'
   Elaine explained that she didn't hear the phone because she ..... to records.
3. Tony: 'I'd send a telegram if I were you.'
   Tony remarked that he ..... send a telegram if he ..... me.
4. Mike: 'I think Dennis will help us.'
   Mike thinks that Dennis ..... help us. Shall we ask him?
5. Carol: 'I think Eric would help, too. Let's ask him.'
   Carol thought that Eric ....., too. She suggested that we should ask him.
6. Maria: 'Dennis could have helped us last night. He would have had time. He just didn't want to.'
   Maria believed that Dennis ..... us last night. She thought he ..... time, but that he just ..... to.

Übung 4

Look at these pairs of sentences.

1. a) Janet said you <u>are</u> very nice.
   b) Janet said you <u>were</u> very nice.

Bei welchem Satz würden Sie sich mehr freuen? Warum?

2. a) Dennis asked if we <u>were</u> looking forward to our holiday.
   b) Dennis asked if we <u>are</u> looking forward to our holiday.

Bei welchem Satz weiß man, daß der Urlaub noch bevorsteht?
ist es nicht klar, ob der Urlaub schon vorbei ist?

3. a) Mike told me he <u>loves</u> Angela.
   b) Mike told me he <u>loved</u> Angela.

Bei welchem Satz würde sich Angela eher freuen? Warum?

4. a) Marion told me she <u>was</u> moving to Sheffield.
   b) Marion told me she <u>is</u> moving to Sheffield.

Bei welchem Satz ist man nicht sicher, ob sie noch umziehen will?

§4 Einleitendes Verb im simple past oder past continuous: Veränderungen in der direkten Rede

'I **want** to go home.'
– Mary said she **wanted** to go home, but no-one listened.
– Mary said she **wants** to go home. I'll go with her.

'My bike**'s been stolen**.'
– Dave told me his bike **had been** stolen. He didn't know that his brother had borrowed it.
– Dave told me his bike **has been** stolen. He's going to tell the police.

1. Die Zeiten ändern sich wie folgt, wenn die Handlung oder das Geschehen der direkten Rede vergangen ist und keine Auswirkung auf die Gegenwart hat. (Siehe auch §3.2–4; §4.2).

wörtliche Rede		indirekte Rede
simple present	→	*simple past*
pres. continuous	→	*past continuous*
present perfect	→	*past perfect*
will-future	→	*conditional: would*
am going to	→	*was going to*
is leaving	→	*was leaving*
future perfect (will have)	→	*future in the past (would have)*

Jill: 'I **had** a bad dream last night'
① Jill was saying she **had** a bad dream last night. (Bericht noch am selben Tag)
② Jill was saying she **had/had had** a bad dream the night before. (Bericht einige Tage später)

2. Wenn die wörtliche Rede im *simple past* steht, kann das *simple past* bei der Wiedergabe in der indirekten Rede zu *past perfect* verändert werden. Es unterbleibt aber immer häufiger, besonders dann, wenn der in der wörtlichen Rede ausgedrückte Zustand bzw. Vorgang nicht so lange her ist (vgl. §3.4).

a) Jill: 'I **don't smoke**.'
– Ben: 'I thought you **didn't smoke**.' (= but now you are smoking)

b) Sue: '**I'm doing** my homework.'
– Mother: You told me you **were doing** your homework, but you're listening to records!

c) Derek: '**I've** just **done** the shopping.'
– Father: I thought Ben **had done** the shopping. But we've no eggs and I can't see any butter!

d) Lynne: '**I'm coming** tomorrow.'
– Mike: You said you **were coming** tomorrow. Why have you changed your mind?

3. Um auf Widersprüche, Fehlinformation und nicht eingehaltene Versprechen hinzuweisen, werden *simple present* (a), *present continuous* (b), *present perfect* (c) und *future* (d) bei der Wiedergabe geändert (vgl. §3.4)

!

'You said you don't smoke.'
(= I suppose that is still true.)

Übung 5

Think carefully about these sentences before completing them, using the verbs in brackets.

1. Linda: 'I'm taking a computer course.'
   Linda told me that (take)
   a) she ..... a computer course. She seems to like it.
   b) she ..... a computer course. But that was several months ago. She might be doing something different now.

2. Wendy: 'I'll be very busy next week.'
   Wendy warned me that (be)
   a) she ..... very busy the following week.
   b) she ..... very busy next week.

3. Ken: 'I saw Sue at a party a few nights ago.'
   Ken told me that (see)
   a) he ..... Sue a few nights ago.
   b) he ..... Sue a few nights before.

§5 Die modalen Hilfsverben in der indirekten Rede

1.a) Die modalen Hilfsverben bleiben bestehen, wenn die Aussage zum Zeitpunkt des Berichtens noch zutrifft bzw. bevorsteht.

Jeff: 'I **can't** come tonight.'
– Jeff said he **can't** come tonight.

b) Wenn aber der Zeit- und Situationsbezug der wörtlichen Rede ein anderer ist, so werden die Hilfsverben wie folgt geändert::

can → could *shall → should*
may → might *will → would*

Steve: 'The TV **won't** work.'
– Steve said the TV **won't** work.
(= it still won't)
Steve said the TV **wouldn't** work.
(= but now it's alright)

2.a) *Must* zum Ausdruck einer Annahme:
Bleibt in der indirekten Rede unverändert.

'All the windows are closed. Ted **must be** out.'
– We decided that Ted **must be** out because all the windows were closed.

b) Verpflichtung, eines Zwanges:
Wenn die Notwendigkeit immer noch besteht, bleibt *must/have to* erhalten.
Besteht die Notwendigkeit nicht mehr, so wird sie durch *had to, would have to, should* ersetzt.

The doctor told my father that he **must** stop smoking.
Ten years ago the doctor told my father that he **had to** stop smoking. So he did.

Diese Regel gilt auch für *need*:

Mother: 'You **needn't come** with me if you don't want to.'

Die Situation der direkten Rede besteht noch.
Mother said I **needn't go** with her.

Der Zeitbezug der indirekten Rede ist ein anderer.
Mother said I **didn't have to** go with her.

Übung 6

Complete these sentences by choosing the correct verb from the box. Which rules helped you to choose?

might — should (2) — should have — must — mustn't

1. 'You should wear a tie tonight.'
a) My girlfriend thought I ..... wear a tie tonight. Are you going to wear one?
b) My girlfriend thought I ..... worn a tie tonight. Everyone else did.

2. 'I may be late, so don't wait for me.'
Derek warned us that he ..... be late, so we didn't wait for him.

3. 'You mustn't forget to send me a postcard.'
a) Martin said we ..... forget to send him a postcard when we go on holiday.
b) Martin said we ..... send him a postcard, but we forgot.

Übung 7

I'd like to introduce the friends you said I could invite for lunch

What do you think the little boy's mother said?

This cartoon is an example of rule § .....

§ 6 Veränderungen bei Pronomina, Zeit- und Ortsangaben, Fragen

Martin: 'Do **you** like **my** new hairstyle?'
– Martin asked **me** if **I** like/liked **his** new hairstyle.

1. Personal- und Possessivpronomina müssen an die veränderte Situation des Berichts angepaßt werden.

'Which do you want, **this** one or **that** one?'
– The assistant asked Neil if he wanted **the blue sweater** or **the yellow one**.

2. Demonstrativpronomina
Manches, was in der wörtlichen Rede offensichtlich ist, muß beim Berichten näher erklärt werden, z. B. wer spricht mit wem (§ 6,1) oder worauf beziehen sich Wörter wie *this, it* usw.

Joe: 'I can't come **tonight**.'
– Joe said he can't come **tonight**. (gleicher Zeitbezug)
– Joe phoned this morning. He said he couldn't come **last night** because his car broke down. (anderer Zeitbezug)

Mary: 'I'm going to New York **this summer**.'
– Mary told me she is/was going to New York **this/that summer/last year/in 1986**.

3. Zeitangaben werden wie folgt geändert, wenn der Zeitbezug der Berichtssituation anders ist als der der wörtlichen Rede. Wenn der Zeitbezug aber noch zutrifft, bleiben die Zeitangaben unverändert.

– *now*	– *at that time/then*
– *today*	– *that day/last Sunday)/ on (May 2/Friday)*
– *yesterday*	– *the day before/last . . ./ on (Tuesday)*
– *tomorrow*	– *the next day/last . . . . ./ on . . . . .*
– *this week*	– *that week*
– *last month*	– *the previous month/the month before/last . . . ./ in (May)*
– *a few days ago*	– *a few days before/ last . . . . ./ on . . . . .*
– *next year*	– *the next year/the following year/in . . . . .*

Brian: 'I'm glad to be **here**.'
– Brian said he was glad to be **back home/in Scotland/with his friends . . . . .**

4. Ortsangaben werden nur dann geändert, wenn der Ortsbezug der wörtlichen Rede nicht zutrifft. Meistens muß eine nähere Erklärung gegeben werden.

Mother: '**How much** did the record cost?'
– My mother **wanted to know how much** the record cost.

Diane: '**What shall** I do?'
– Diane didn't know **what to do**.

5. Fragen mit Fragewörtern und mit *shall* werden als indirekte Fragen wiedergegeben.

Ann: 'Do you watch TV much?'
– Ann asked **if** I watch TV much.

Ann: 'Do you prefer to read or watch TV?'
– Ann asked **whether/(if)** I prefer/preferred to read or watch TV.

6. Für Entscheidungsfragen braucht man in der indirekten Rede *if/whether.*
If klingt informeller. *Whether* steht oft bei Entscheidungsfragen.
Häufige Verben: *ask, wonder, not know, want to know.*

Übung 8

Use the box to report what these people said or did.

1. Carol ..... a boy .....
2. Jeff offered to look after ..... cat while she is on holiday.
3. Tom told me that Barbara is starting her new job .....
4. I met Alan in town last week. He said that he had met a fantastic girl ..... and that he was taking her out .....
5. Linda invited Joe to her party .....
6. Kevin ..... we are going with him.

- the next day
- wanted to know
- last week
- standing near the window
- if
- on Monday
- the night before
- pointed to
- Mrs Smith's

Training
Aufsatz
Erzählen
Nacherzählen

Training
100 Diktate
4. Schuljahr

PC-Kombi-Training
Übungs-CD-ROM und Lernbuch
Englisch
7. Schuljahr

LEKTÜREHILFEN
Nathan der Weise

ABITUR
WISSEN
Landeskunde
Great Britain
United States of America

ABI-Training
Geschichte